Skateboarding to the EXTREME!

ENCINITAS SKATER MIDAIR APPROACHING A HANDRAIL.

Skateboarding TO the EXTREME!

Bill Gutman

A Tom Doherty Associates Book / New York

A Tor® Book
Published by Tom Doherty Associates, Inc.
175 Fifth Avenue
New York, NY 10010

Tor® is a registered trademark of Tom Doherty Associates, Inc.

Library of Congress Cataloging-in-Publication Data

Gutman, Bill.
    Skateboarding : to the extreme! / Bill Gutman.
        p.   cm.
    "A Tom Doherty Associates book."
    ISBN 0-312-86153-2
    1. Skateboarding.   I. Title.
GV859.8.G88   1997
796.22—dc21   97-6278
                                      CIP

First Edition: May 1997

Printed in the United States of America

0 9 8 7 6 5 4 3

6/99 BCT

ACKNOWLEDGMENTS

For their help and contributions to *Skateboarding: To the Extreme!*
Tor Books gives special thanks to:

World Industries
Oakley Sunglasses, Inc.
Rector Safety Gear
Rodney Mullen
Mike McGill
Henry Hester
Tony Hawk and his dad, Frank, for the use of their ramps.

CONTENTS

INTRODUCTION

SINCE the early 1960s, skateboarding has been many things to many people. It has been alternately a cross-training tool, a competitive sport, an almost cultlike activity, and a way of life. Perhaps no other outdoor activity has had as many ups and downs, slumps and comebacks, and such a constant flux of what's "in" and what's "out" as skateboarding.

Each succeeding generation of skateboarders seems to bring its own style and substance along with it, often rejecting what came before. This has resulted in the feeling that skateboarding is "starting all over" every five or ten years. In a way, this kind of inconsistency has hurt skateboarding's overall development. It has prevented skateboarding from being an organized, nationwide sport. Without a strong national organization to set parameters and guidelines, the sport has sometimes suffered. Yet devoted skateboarders seem to like things just the way they are. One top skater, for instance, explained it this way:

"If you put skateboarding in the Olympics, you would destroy it."

Skateboarding is not about to go to the Olympics. In fact, at the beginning of the 1990s, it had become more of a street sport than anything else. Streetstyle is the "in" kind of skating. Slalom and downhill racing are a thing of the past. Vertical skating (half-pipe and pool) is on the wane. Flatland freestyle has become an anachronism. Most newer skaters are not interested in hill-riding, barrel-, or high-jumping.

All these activities have played a big part in the growth of skateboarding over the years. But instead of being organized and remaining a viable and competitive part of the sport, they have become obsolete. However, because of the changing nature of skateboarding, activities such as slalom and downhill racing may not be buried forever.

For that reason, this book will represent a comprehensive study of skateboarding, including not only what is happening now, but what has come before and might happen again. It will discuss all aspects of the sport, including those activities not considered to be "in" at the time of this writing. There is no reason that youngsters just beginning to skate should not be aware of all the possibilities that skateboarding offers them.

If they want to try the slalom, why not? If they want the excitement of taking a hill, why not? If they want to perform some flatland freestyle, they should know how. And if they want to organize a series of competitive races, they ought to do it. They shouldn't be stopped by what is perceived as the only way to go.

Skateboarding is too versatile an activity to be pigeonholed in a corner. Yes, the sport has been many things to many people since it began. There's no reason why it can't be that way again.

PART ONE

RODNEY MEAD, STIFFIE INVERT, MCGILL'S SKATE PARK.

A SKATEBOARDING HISTORY

THE concept of skateboarding is such a simple one that it's amazing it wasn't discovered much earlier. After all, roller skating became a real sport in the 1860s, nearly one hundred years before the first skateboards began to appear. So it's pretty safe to say that someone must have tinkered with a broken pair of roller skates and attached the wheels to a solid board back then.

That's actually how the first boards appeared. They were homemade creations that probably didn't last very long. There are reports of crude skateboards appearing as early as the 1930s or 1940s. Certainly, there must have been some boards appearing in the 1950s, especially in the warm-weather climates of Florida and California.

Henry Hester, who would someday become a world champion in the skateboard slalom competition, remembers his first skateboard:

"My dad took a piece of two-by-four and nailed some roller-skate wheels onto it," Hester said. "It was maybe twenty-two inches long, only four inches wide, and real simple. I guess I was in junior high school then and a number of my friends had similar homemade boards."

That was in the early 1960s and just about the time the first skateboard revolution was beginning to take place. It all started as a crossover activity. California surfers saw the skateboard as a way to practice their primary sport during bad weather or even at home when they couldn't get to the beach. So the first skateboards were substitute surfboards.

Sidewalk surfing became a fad in California around 1962 and lasted about three years. There was even a hit song about it by the then-popular duo Jan and Dean. For the first time, several companies began to manufacture skateboards and the first boards sold like hotcakes. One estimate said that by 1965, there had been some fifty million skateboards sold in the United States.

"We would paint little dots on the streets and slalom in and out of the dots," Henry Hester recalls. "By then we had manufactured boards, but sometimes still fooled around making our own. We made the boards out of plywood and bought what they called 'super surfer' boards that had clay wheels. Sometimes we would glue sandpaper on the tail of the board so we wouldn't slip off and we started doing wheelies and things like that."

But the skateboarding fad of the mid-1960s was short-lived. It crested in 1965, then took a nosedive. There were a number of reasons cited for the rapid decline. The quality of the early boards was not good. Many snapped under the pressure of heavy usage and more daring skaters. The boards were flat and not designed nearly as well as later models. In addition, the small, clay wheels couldn't handle rough surfaces and skaters often wiped out if they hit a rough patch of sidewalk or road. Besides poor traction, the boards simply didn't have enough mobility.

At the same time, the public perception of skateboarding had soured. The sound of the wheels on concrete surfaces was noisy and harsh on the ears. With skateboards cruising up and down the sidewalks, weaving in and out of pedestrians, more people began to fear they would be slammed into by an out-of-control skater. They didn't want to compete for sidewalk space with these often daring and quick skaters.

The fear factor went a step further when the California Medical Association released statistics that showed skateboarding accidents were becoming more prevalent than bicycle accidents as a major cause of injuries to children. In addition, nearly one-third of skateboarding injuries involved adults.

With all of that, a backlash against the sport developed rapidly. Many cities from coast to coast began to pass ordinances that banned skateboarding on public streets and sidewalks. And at the same time the youngsters seemed to lose interest. Too many accidents; too many broken boards. The kids and young adults all seemed to quit around the same time. Like the Hula-Hoop, skateboarding was looked upon as a fad that had come and gone with breakneck speed.

"Hardly anyone skated after 1965 or 1966," Henry Hester remembers. "It had been almost solely a sidewalk sport then. But I remember seeing an early movie about that time called *Skater-Dater*. It was a boy-meets-girl, boy-leaves-girl kind of movie and all the kids were skating barefooted, going downhill.

"There were even some early big names then. We all knew about Torger Johnson, Bruce Logan and Davey Hilton from Hilton Hotel fame. For awhile, we skated every day. Then it just faded away."

There was even a new skateboarding magazine that came out about that time. It lasted just four issues and folded. Skateboarding was out.

The status quo didn't change until 1973. The biggest initial innovation in the comeback of skateboarding was the use of urethane wheels. Urethane is a soft, durable plastic that was used on roller-skate wheels first. These wheels were softer than clay and as a result gripped the skating surface better. But they were also slower and roller skaters didn't like them. With skates on both feet, roller skaters didn't have the same traction problems that skateboarders had.

Fortunately, the wheels weren't discarded. It took a surfer named Frank Nasworthy to think of using urethane wheels on skateboards. Nasworthy was from Encinitas, California, and before long his idea was put to use by several skateboarding companies. Urethane wheels gave the skaters a safer, smoother ride. Combined with new, flexible fiberglass boards, skaters now had a piece of equipment they could push to its limits. Skateboarding began to take off once again.

This time the sport really grew quickly. It wasn't just a bunch of kids surfing on the sidewalks. This time it had a real sense of purpose and organization. Skateboard parks began opening around the country—places where people could go and skate half-pipes, in bowls, and on ramps. They could practice downhill and slalom racing or just plain have fun.

There were more competitive contests springing up all over, with skaters competing in downhill racing, slalom racing, cross-country, bowl-riding, and freestyle. More and more youngsters took up the new sport and many became outstanding skateboarders in a relatively short period of time.

By 1976, skateboarding had become a $300 million-a-year business, with both large corporations and small entrepreneurs turning out skateboards at a fast pace.

Rodney Mullen, who would become a world-champion freestyler, began skating at about this very time.

"My father was a doctor and was fearful that I would get hurt on a skateboard," Mullen said. "But finally in January of 1977 he relented and bought me my first board. I was just ten at the time and thought skateboarding was a cool thing to do."

Mullen was so good at it and practiced so much that within two years he won the amateur championship of California and a year later was a world champion in freestyling. He was just thirteen years old at the time.

Mike McGill began skating on a borrowed board when he was nearly twelve. He began on his driveway in Florida and before long had his own board and was building a driveway ramp. From there it was on to a skate park in Tampa, Florida, where he began to excel at vertical skating. Before his fourteenth birthday he was representing his park in contests against other skate parks in the area.

"Back then there was a lot of bowl-riding, flatland freestyle, and snake runs, which was like a cross-country course," McGill said. "This was about 1980 and stuff like the downhill and slalom was already starting to die out by then."

Mike McGill would become a world champion at vertical skating (ramps and bowls), but by that time the sport was changing once again. In the early 1980s, skateboarding inexplicably went into another down period. This one is tough even for guys like Mullen and McGill to explain. It just seemed to happen. Not many youngsters were taking up the sport. But then in the mid-to-late 1980s it began growing once more, and spread to Europe and to the Scandinavian countries, even to Australia.

"I remember about 1985 and 1986 I began going out on a lot of tours, giving demos all over the place," said Mullen. "By 1986, it was huge again and we were all stars."

It was the age of the VCR and skateboarding videos were popping up all over, enabling more and more youngsters to observe the sport in their own living rooms. There were new and better skateboards, with new ideas and new models being tried and sometimes discarded. But the latest boom didn't last, either.

The sport was changing again. It had been a real speed sport during the boom of the mid-1970s. Skaters were running hills, racing in the downhill and slalom and over cross-country courses, trying to beat the fastest time. But by the time of the resurgence of the mid-1980s, most of the speed aspects of the sport had disappeared. New skaters were more interested in technique, and streetstyle slowly evolved.

In the early 1990s, skateboarding was in another state of flux. Once again interest dropped, though not to the extent it had during the other down periods. One of the problems was the disappearance of many skate parks. Problems with liability insurance and lack of interest caused many to close. And many towns and cities still ban skating on most public sidewalks and parking lots. Sometimes a kid just doesn't have a lot of places to skate.

The disappearance of the popular early disciplines (downhill, slalom, flatland freestyle) has eliminated many choices for skaters. The most popular style of skating in the early 1990s is streetstyle. That can be very technical and sometimes devoid of movement.

"I've seen a group of maybe six, seven, or ten skaters just working on one structure or obstacle," said Henry Hester. "Maybe it's a pipe, a curb, or a handrailing. But they'll just stay there and work that thing for two or three hours, trying different technical tricks."

Skateboarding remains ever-changing and evolving. Its history is by no means complete. Because of the unpredictable nature of the sport, there is always a chance that future skaters will once again fly down hills, or zigzag their way through a slalom course or simply perfect new flatland freestyle routines. For that reason, none of those skating techniques should be forgotten.

For in skateboarding, the next chapter in its history could begin tomorrow.

ORGANIZED SKATEBOARDING

Skateboarding today is a very loosely organized sport, so much so that it may be more accurately described as simply an activity. This may not sound encouraging to newcomers or even to those who have given years to spreading the word and trying to foster increased participation in skateboarding. But the organization or lack of organization has been the result of the uneven history of the sport.

For example, there were once many organized downhill and slalom races throughout the United States. That's how Henry Hester became a champion. But with the decline in downhill and slalom riding by new skateboarders, the competition and organized contests have also disappeared. You can't hold a competition if no one wants to compete.

Flatland freestyle competition is what made Rodney Mullen a champion. In the 1990s, flatland has been replaced by streetstyle. Unless the former flatlanders want to move over to streetstyle, they will no longer be a part of any overall or national organization.

Streetstyle skaters are often technically brilliant. They can do an outstanding number of tricks utilizing natural obstacles such as curbs, handrails, benches, walls—anything that is out on the street. But there is another inherent danger that this style of technical skating presents.

"A lot of kids begin practicing these technical street tricks almost as soon as they get on the board," said Rodney Mullen. "They often end up doing the tricks, but other than that they can't skate at all."

If that's the case, the kids won't ever be able to downhill or slalom, or even skate safely down the street. That's why learning the basics of the sport are so important, and why every aspect will be described in the course of this book.

"I would make every kid starting in the sport learn how to take hills, pop off curbs, really get the feel of the board and not be afraid of a little speed," Mullen continued. "That way he'll get some confidence in what he's doing. He also should be able to switch his stance, push with both his right and left foot. That's important.

"Then when he has all those skills he can begin doing streetstyle tricks if he chooses. With the basic skills he'll learn the tricks much faster and really be able to tear them apart."

Further evidence that the uneven evolution of the sport has hurt it nationally comes from Henry Hester in speaking about the National Skateboard Association. There was a time when the NSA seemed well on its way to becoming the one governing body for skateboarding. Not so in the early nineties.

"Even in the middle 1980s the NSA was running contests in major areas of the country, putting up lights and constructing lavish ramps," Hester said. "They had a vision of a real big blowout type of thing with a big production. But within five years the NSA has become almost a mom-and-pop type of organization.

"The people who run it move around a lot and don't hold as many contests. When they do, it's become more of a backyard kind of thing. Sometimes, for instance, they'll just have a pool-riding contest in a private backyard and they won't even let many spectators in."

Rodney Mullen said that even the judging of existing contests is not always uniform.

"It's vague," he said. "There's no real system for judging. Most of the judges are older skaters who don't really know the latest tricks and maneuvers. It's difficult for a judge to evaluate a skater doing new tricks that he hasn't seen before. The only positive thing is that somehow it usually works out. The winner is usually the person who deserves to win."

In other words, skateboarders are not required to perform certain set maneuvers or tricks. Figure skaters, for instance, must all do the same compulsory figures before their free-skating program. Skateboarders can pretty much do whatever they please.

The lack of a real organization has also hurt skateboarding in many areas. The result is that many towns and cities continue to ban the sport from public places. In fact, in some small towns, the kids have almost nowhere to skate. They practice tricks in their garages and basements. And while they may become technically proficient, they can't get out in the open spaces and really skate, creating the situation that was described above by Rodney Mullen.

Why is this happening and what can youngsters who want to skate do about it?

Henry Hester feels part of the problem is an old one—the noise level and fear of the unknown.

"The wheels today are harder and noisier," Hester said. "When a group of kids skates down a sidewalk you can really hear it. People who own shops don't want the ruckus and the possibility of skaters running into customers or people walking on the street.

"But that doesn't really happen very often. Skaters usually have pretty good control of what they're doing. If you see a group of five skaters coming toward you there's not much chance you will be hit. In fact, I've never seen anyone on a skateboard hit someone who was walking. Yet I can also see the concern, especially with older people.

"So there's still a kind of prejudice against skateboarders due to the fact that it's noisy and loud."

There have been periods when the image of skateboarders wasn't a good one. Rodney Mullen agrees that the anti-skateboarding feeling isn't always based on fact.

"There's a big bias [against skating] and it's a pain," he said. "There was a time in the eighties when skating was tied to punk rock. It resulted in an image of skaters wearing mohawk hairstyles and looking terrible. I think that negative image has played a big part in skating being banned. Some of the skateboarding magazines didn't help, either.

"But there are plenty of straight, clean-cut kids skating and they shouldn't have to pay the price."

There have also been cases, however, where young skaters don't show much regard for private property. Doing their maneuvers against a bench or a wooden planter, or even a piece of soft marble, can cause damage.

And as Henry Hester said, many skaters don't have an appreciation for property because of their age.

The problem of liability insurance has also caused other public places—like parking lots and playgrounds—to ban the boards. It seems strange in that kids have been riding bicycles in these places for years. Anyone can certainly take a bad fall from a bike. But bikes have been around a long time. They are almost part of the landscape. Skateboarding is not.

Again, the solution in a rather loosely knit sport seems to be in one word: Organize.

"In my city, Carlsbad, California, they recently tried banning skateboards from the streets," said vertical-skating champ Mike McGill. "But they left it up to the property owners to post signs if they didn't want skating on their property. So I tell young kids to stay away from areas that are posted.

"But people should try to organize. Kids should get their parents involved. Liability is a problem. No one wants to pay for it. Yet if there are enough kids skating and they have their parents behind them, they should be able to get their city or town to build a place for them to skate. After all, look at all the baseball and football fields around.

"Kids can also go to organizations like the YMCA or Boys and Girls Clubs for help. We don't have enough places now, but if you go through organizations, or have a group of parents speak to the city councils and explain the situation, it can help. How can you allow a kid to ride a bicycle but not a skateboard? What's the difference?"

Henry Hester said that skating was banned in many places in Virginia Beach, California, but that many of the surf shops and businesses that were losing money because of it got together and built a public facility for skaters.

"That's kind of rare right now," Hester said, "but it proves it can be done. The parents helped, too."

Rodney Mullen feels that skateboarding will always be on the edge and never be a fully organized nationwide sport.

"The image just isn't good," he said. "In fact, over the years many of the skateboarding magazines have tended to push the eccentric character of the sport. For those reasons you'll never see it in the Olympics. Yet it's come back to cleaner kids in recent years, without the attitudes and attempts to be cool. There's a lot of normal kids out there who like to skate and they should have a place to do it."

The image Rodney Mullen refers to is that of an outlaw sport where kids often defy authority, skating in prohibited areas and then using their skating skills to flee. Some have indeed seemed to revel in that image. But you will get people like that in any activity.

It seems the key should be playing by the book. Don't flout the rules or the law in order to skate. Instead organize, get together, form a town club or group. Then find a sponsor, maybe a group of parents or some local businessmen. Make a sincere and honest appeal for a place to skate, citing the healthful merits of the sport and the desire of your group to participate together. Maybe even organize some local contests and try to get others interested as spectators.

Skaters won't serve themselves or the sport well by going it alone, by being maverick athletes who flout the rules and rebel. It won't work if they want skateboarding to grow slowly and evenly. If the organization is strong the word will get out. More youngsters will try skating and become interested in the activity. Then, maybe skateboarding will be able to avoid the ups and down that have characterized its history and sabotaged its attempts to organize on state and national levels.

PART TWO

RON YERMAN SMITH-GRINDS HIS BACKYARD RAMP.

GETTING READY TO SKATE

THE SKATEBOARD

SKATEBOARDS have come a long way since the days of the two-by-fours with the roller-skate wheels nailed to them. Down through the years the boards have changed, not always for the better. Rodney Mullen recalls the sometimes strange evolution of the skateboard.

"It seemed as if anything new would become exaggerated," he said. "The boards started out very, very thin, maybe six or seven inches wide. Then they began growing up to maybe ten to twelve inches wide. By that time, they were all flat with a slight kick [rise] in the tail [the rear of the board].

"Then concave boards began coming in, just slightly concave to hold your feet a little better so you knew where your feet were all the time. But then it went to extremes again and boards came out that you could almost take a bath in. Finally, they began making them with double kicks, symmetrical boards with the nose and tail the same.

"The boards today for the most part are slightly concave with a double kick, and about nine inches wide."

Wheels have also changed to accommodate the different styles of skating that have come and gone over the years. The biggest change was the shift from clay to urethane. After that, wheels began to differ in size. They started small, then got bigger when the emphasis was on speed. Now they are small again, about 40–45 mm. Because skating has become very technical without the emphasis on speed, the wheels aren't real fast but give the skaters the quickness they need.

Over the years, skateboards were made of a variety of materials. During the boom period of the mid-1970s to early 1980s, the old stiff wooden boards were discarded in favor of something called "flexboards." These boards were an improvement on the older models in that they absorbed road shock much better. They could also be made to speed up or slow down simply by the skater applying more weight on the board (pressing down hard) for speed and taking weight off for slowing.

Flexboards were often made of fiberglass, aluminum, or plastic, getting away from the solid, one-piece wood boards that had been so rigid earlier. But as the skaters continued to improve, they found fault with all three styles of construction.

Fiberglass at first seemed like a perfect solution. The boards were sturdy and very flexible. But the more skaters used them, the more they realized that the ride wasn't even as smooth as with the old wooden boards. In addition, the boards were heavy and could be easily damaged if they took a pounding.

The answer wasn't aluminum. These boards were expensive and could be very attractive when new. But a sidewalk skater would often scrape the

1 WORLD INDUSTRIES, JEREMY KLEIN MODEL SKATEBOARD, THE CONTEMPORARY
FORM OF BOARDS TO DATE, ALSO WITH VENTURE TRUCKS AND JASON LEE
WHEELS.

boards against curbs and the pavement, creating jagged edges that could give the skater a nasty cut.

Plastic was the most inexpensive of the three and, for awhile, a good board for beginners. But many of these boards would begin to sag after repeated use and would also become soft if left in the hot sun. By contrast, cold weather made them brittle and prone to cracking. Even beginners soon had to get a second board.

All that changed when the modern wooden skateboard was developed in the mid-1980s. Now, a good skateboard is tough and durable. As with all sports that require a special piece of equipment, beginning skateboarders should buy the very best quality board they can afford. If they care for it, it will serve them well for a long time.

The top skateboards today are made by layering thin pieces of a quality hardwood together. The wood is usually maple, oak, or beech and the board can consist of up to seven plys of the wood glued together. These boards are very durable, yet lightweight and flexible. They combine all the good qualities of the boards that came before. Plywood boards can be used by all types of skaters, though with the aforementioned smaller wheels, they aren't really built for speed.

Most skaters prefer a board with a double *kick,* a gradual rise on both ends of the board, though boards with a kick in just the tail are still made. The flat surface of the board is called the *deck.* Most skaters involved with streetstyle and ramp riding prefer a board from 9 to 11 inches wide and 29 to 32 inches long. Beginners may prefer to start with a smaller board that will give them better control as they learn the various techniques.

There are several other important working parts to a board that all skaters should know about. The suspension systems on which the wheels are mounted are called *trucks.* They are made from a strong metal and include built-in shock pads to absorb the bumps and jumps of streetstyle skating.

Today's wheels are made solely from urethane. It gives the skater better traction, absorbs the shock of a rough surface, and allows for sharp turns with less danger of a wipeout. So urethane wheels are safer and last longer than the old clay wheels. The wheels used for most streetstyle and freestyle skating are about 1⅛ inches wide and 1½ inches in diameter. These wheels don't grip as well at higher speeds. So anyone interested in downhill or slalom racing should get a larger wheel, one about 2¼ inches wide and 2⅝ inches in diameter.

When looking to buy a skateboard, always check the wheels. If they don't spin freely or have even the slightest wobble, don't buy that board. Also make sure there are no defects such as high or low spots on the wheel. And if you press down hard on a wheel with your thumb, you should not see any kind of depression mark on the surface of the wheel.

Many of today's wheels contain sealed, lubricated precision ball bearings. The bearings are what give you a good ride. Quality sealed bearings will provide the quietest, smoothest ride on the board. There will be no wobble at all, not even at high speeds or during turns. In addition, they never need maintenance.

Again, look for quality. Champion skateboarder Mike McGill is very adamant about this when asked for advice by newcomers to the sport.

"There are many foreign-made boards that are copies of boards made in the United States," McGill says. "I really think people should avoid these boards. They may be less expensive to buy, but in many cases the trucks are not made correctly and it's much more difficult to turn well on them. Also, the bearings are not always of good quality and can have a tendency to lock up. And that means skaters can get hurt. So I tell people to avoid these types of boards, period.

"Start with a top-quality skateboard and you'll learn faster, as well as enjoy the sport more."

CARE AND MAINTENANCE

As with any good piece of sporting equipment, skateboards should be kept in tip-top shape at all times. To take your board for granted can be expensive and can get you hurt. Make sure the deck of your board is always clean and dry after you use it. Just warm water and maybe a mild soap is all that is needed to get mud, grit, or road grime off your board. When you finish, be certain the board is dry.

Otherwise, about the only other thing you have to watch for is cracks in the wood. You wouldn't want your board to snap during a difficult or potentially dangerous stunt. However, the modern, layered boards will rarely snap. Nor do they often crack. But they should be inspected after each use for any signs of cracking. Slight cracks may be repaired at a skateboard shop before they get any worse. But a bad crack usually means you'll need a new deck.

Wheels, of course, should always be inspected for defects and signs of wear. Urethane wheels last much longer than the old clay wheels. In addition, always make sure all your wheels spin freely. If they don't, it may simply be a matter of the bearing race nut on the wheel being too tight. Back off on the nut slowly until the wheel once again spins with no resistance.

One other trick to extend wheel life: If you skate often, make sure to rotate your wheels about once a month. This is similar to rotating the tires on a car. The best way to rotate skate wheels is to switch the left front with the right rear wheel, and the right front with the left rear wheel. This will allow for even wear and longer life.

If you have sealed wheel bearings they will never need maintenance. However, if you have wheels with loose or open bearings (these are still used on some inexpensive boards), you'll have to be sure to keep them clean. This can be done by obtaining a special bearing spray, which will remove any grit or dirt that has collected in the bearings.

It is also important to check the truck bolt, making sure that it is tight enough to prevent any wheel wobble. There should always be pressure between the bolt and truck plate. A special skate key can be obtained to tighten this bolt. It's small enough for skaters to carry with them at all times.

Trucks should be kept clean and free from rust. They can be wiped down with a damp cloth to remove dirt, then dried and wiped again with a light oil or lubricant to keep corrosion down. The position of the trucks on the underside of the deck can also be adjusted. A long wheelbase, with the trucks near the ends of the board, is better for someone who likes speed and favors downhill riding.

The long wheelbase also gives the board more flexibility. But a short wheelbase, with the trucks mounted closer to the middle of the board, makes it easier to do technical maneuvers such as wheelies and kickturns. Freestylers and streetstylers prefer the shorter wheelbase.

There is not a whole lot of maintenance involved with a skateboard, just the few basic things that have been outlined here. However, they are important. Don't neglect your skateboard and think it will last forever. A little preventive maintenance will go a long way.

CLOTHING AND PROTECTIVE GEAR

In any kind of sport involving wheels and speed, participants should try to protect themselves from injury any way they can. With skateboarding, this means wearing certain pieces of protective gear. Unfortunately, skateboarders don't always follow this advice.

Down through the years, it hasn't always been considered "cool" to wear protective clothing and gear. This is especially true out on the streets. Instead of a helmet, kneepads, and elbow pads, kids will go out in whatever outfit they prefer to be seen in that day.

Another problem is that skateboarding has always been popular in warm-weather states such as Florida and California. In very muggy weather, protective gear can make a skater even hotter and more uncomfortable. So shorts and a T-shirt—and sometimes even bare feet—can be the standard skating apparel even when the tricks and maneuvers have an element of risk.

Of course, skaters involved in competition or in riding ramps and pools at skate parks are required to wear protective gear. But street skaters should be sure to take heed when deciding how to dress for a robust skating session. And beginners shouldn't even think twice about wearing protective gear. They should just do it.

The gear for skateboarders isn't extensive. Begin with the helmet. For years, there were no special helmets made for skateboards. It was really a matter of any good helmet would do. Some skaters wore motorcycle helmets, some wore helmets designed for bicycle riders, while others even donned football or hockey helmets.

All of this gear offers protection. The bicycle helmet is probably closer to the helmets made for skateboarders today. Helmets made for related wheeled sports such as in-line skating are also fine for skateboarding and similar to the helmets some of the skateboarding manufacturers now turn out.

Skateboarding helmets are lightweight, with the shell made of a durable plastic. They are lined with Styrofoam padding, and are vented in both the front and rear. No helmet is going to be completely comfortable in hot, humid weather. But new skaters can easily get used to these lightweight protectors so that they become part of their everyday skating outfit.

The helmet is probably the single most important piece of protective equipment a skateboarder can wear, especially when he is involved in high-speed or high-flying maneuvers. But there are some other pieces of gear he should consider as well.

Kneepads, elbow pads, as well as palm and wrist guards, will also keep skateboarders from getting a whole variety of scrapes, bumps, and bruises.

An article in a weekend newsmagazine in early 1992 contained a short piece on athletic injuries for the nineties. One short section was addressed to skateboarders. It talked about a "wrist slam," "chin skin," and "hipper," all injuries related to boarding. But the most painful was called a "swell-bow," in which the sac protecting the elbow fills with fluid after repeated bangs and knocks.

Most of these injuries can be avoided by the use of protective equipment. Good knee and elbow pads manufactured today are reinforced with a plastic cap filled with foam padding. These will cushion blows even more than the old style which simply had the foam padding without the cap. But even those are better than nothing.

Wrist guards are made with a metal bar that helps protect both the palm and the wrist. The bar is shaped to the contour of the hand and wrist

2 RECTOR SAFETY GEAR SHOWS THEIR HELMET, KNEE AND ELBOW GUARDS ALONG WITH THEIR WRIST GUARDS.

and can not only prevent a scrape or bad bruise, but also a potential broken wrist. Optional gear includes padded pants to protect the thighs and hip pads to prevent the aforementioned "hipper" injury.

As mentioned earlier, the changing and sometimes fickle nature of this sport has often dictated that protective gear isn't cool. Like a lot of the older forms of the sport (downhill, slalom), the use of helmets and pads is considered "out." Newcomers to skateboarding should not be influenced by this kind of thinking. It's never cool to get hurt. Protective gear should be just as important as your skateboard. Use it.

SAFETY AND PITFALLS

As with any sport, newcomers to skateboarding should be aware of what safety measures they must take to avoid possible pitfalls when learning new skills and then becoming more advanced. We have already talked about taking care of your skateboard and wearing protective gear. That's step one when it comes to basic skateboarding safety.

But there are other measures to take as well. For instance, the new skater (as well as an experienced one) should know where, and where not, to skate. The best place, obviously, is an area designated for skateboarding, such as a skateboarding park, an empty playground, or parking lot. But in the early 1990s, there were far fewer skating parks than in the mid-1980s. So, in a sense, there are fewer places to skate.

That can sometimes leave a skater with tough choices. If skateboarders are allowed to skate on a public sidewalk they should be sure to watch out for pedestrians. Nothing will get skaters banned more quickly than if they constantly cut off, collide with, or injure pedestrians. Be sure to avoid pedestrians. Give them the right of way and skate safety.

If you are skating on the street you must obey all traffic signs, signals, and regulations. Otherwise, you'll be a menace to yourself, pedestrians, and perhaps even automobiles. And again, careless and unsafe skating will result in a ban.

Picking a street on which to skate also takes some common sense. There is much more chance of an accident if you skate on a busy, traffic-filled street with cars coming from every direction. A quiet, country road is a much better choice whenever possible. But even then skaters must stay alert for automobiles, runners, and even bicyclists.

Another rule of thumb is never to skate at night. Even with bright, reflective clothing there are still too many pitfalls. You can't always see the skating surface adequately and perhaps will not be able to judge distance as well. Plus you can easily be blinded by the headlights of oncoming cars, even if you are on the sidewalk. And without reflective clothing, a car may not be able to see you.

Skateboarders—like roller skaters and bicyclists—are sometimes tempted to grab onto and allow another vehicle to pull them along. This can be extremely dangerous, especially if the other vehicle is motorized. This is something that even the most experienced and talented street skater should never do. It's asking for trouble and those who ask for trouble usually find it.

Should you suddenly come across an emergency situation that could result in an injury, you've got to be ready. The most obvious way to avoid many pitfalls is to perfect your skill as a skateboarder. If you always have control over the board, you can avoid encountering many kinds of problems.

Good control will enable you to avoid pedestrians and possibly even automobiles. Skaters, however, would be wise to stay away from situations where they might have to dodge autos. Control of the board will also enable skaters to recover if they should run across an obstacle on the sidewalk, road, or parking lot.

However, there are going to be situations in which every skater, no matter how good, will have to leave the board. Sometimes, he can just hop off. But other times he is going to fall. Knowing how to fall correctly is very important. Falling on flat land or while doing street tricks is a bit different from taking a spill during vertical (half-pipe or pool) skating.

Again, the safest and easiest way to get off the board is to simply hop off. You can generally do this if the board isn't moving too fast. Since many streetstyle maneuvers are done at a relatively slow speed, skaters can usually dismount and land on their feet. Of course, there will be times when they may not land squarely on the board and a fall is inevitable.

Professional skater Mike McGill is one who advocates the use of wrist guards when skating on ramps and even doing maneuvers like riding handrails on the streets.

"Wrist injuries are very common," McGill said. "I see a lot of guys on the ramps as well as the street guys wearing wrist guards now. Skaters who are pushing along on flat ground or maybe working up a little speed are more likely to fall backwards if they wipe out."

A skater who feels himself falling should try to fall so that one of the fleshier parts of his body absorbs most of the impact. That's step one. The second part of a fall is to try to distribute the impact over as much of the body as possible, rather than just any one part. This is generally done by twisting and then rolling.

If you feel you are going to fall forward, start by dropping your body lower to the ground, bending at the knees if you can. This will decrease the distance you will actually fall and will lessen the impact. At the moment of impact, lower your head and turn it away from the direction of the fall. Then tuck your lead arm and shoulder in so you can roll. The momentum should carry you over. Depending on your speed, you can roll two or three times rather than try to stop the roll. To stop it can result in a slide and some nasty abrasions.

During a backwards fall, twist your body to the side to absorb the impact with your leg and hip, rather than your back or head. With practice, it's also possible to go into a roll from a backward fall. These techniques should be practiced before you actually begin skating at faster speeds.

3 MIKE MCGILL SHOWING THE PROPER WAY TO FALL FROM A TRICK.

One other tip. When falling, don't allow your body to stiffen. This can cause a greater impact and make it difficult to turn and roll. Stay loose and relaxed. That way, you'll be able to roll with the punches much easier.

Ramp or pool-riding requires a different kind of falling technique, especially when you are at the top of the ramp or are starting back down. The object is to land on both knees (with high-quality kneepads, of course) and to simply slide down the ramp.

If you're riding a ramp and feel yourself losing contact with the board, immediately try to stabilize your body by using your hands for balance. Then immediately bring your knees together and put them into a tuck position. Try to ease down to the skating surface as quickly as you can.

Should you be airborne and feel you won't return to the board, again stabilize as best you can. Sometimes you might have to hit with your feet, then drop immediately to your knees for the slide. To come down directly on both knees can create a nasty impact. The feet-to-knees release will lessen it considerably.

Beginning skaters should make sure to learn the basic rules of skateboard safety as one of the first steps in learning their new sport. They should also talk to more experienced skaters about some of the hazards and pitfalls they might run into along the way. Once they know how to react, they are less likely to be injured when that emergency situation occurs.

FITNESS AND TRAINING

There are varying opinions about the degree of fitness needed to skateboard. Some say to just get on the board and go, that no preliminary work is needed to get ready.

"That's the beauty of skateboarding," Mike McGill has said. "You don't have to be super-fit. You can be fat, skinny, short, or tall. It doesn't matter. For just starting out, no real preparation is necessary. Of course, once you start doing advanced maneuvers, you might want to stretch. But if you just want to skate, you just go."

Henry Hester said that skateboarding in the early 1990s was no longer a "super physical sport. A lot of kids do their tricks standing there. Skiers, for instance, don't see skateboarding as going out and exercising."

Rodney Mullen, on the other hand, says that preliminary exercises aren't mandatory, but that some kind of effort is a good idea.

"Stretching is always a good thing," Mullen said. "There are some other good exercises, as well. For instance, a skater should exercise his shoulders. I used to do a lot of karate. That teaches you your center of balance and flexibility as well. Anything that helps balance and quickness will help in skating. And any discipline that teaches concentration is also a help."

Once again the conflicting opinions seem to stem from the changing styles and attitudes of the sport. What was needed to prepare for downhill and slalom racing years ago isn't really necessary today. But then again, ramp and vertical skating takes some real physical skills and effort. New skaters would be wise to prepare themselves for skateboarding as they would for most any other sport. In other words, be reasonably physically fit before they begin. Then remain that way.

It would not be responsible for this book to suggest that someone should begin to skateboard without first having some degree of fitness. Even if you decide to stop skating, good fitness is forever. That's why it's important to start right.

Any athlete should have a good degree of aerobic fitness. Aerobic exercise conditions the heart and lungs by increasing the body's efficient intake of oxygen. In other words, it gives you more endurance and you don't get tired as quickly. Running, jumping rope, and fast dancing are all examples of aerobic exercise. To increase your endurance, you should exercise aerobically for at least twenty to thirty minutes, nonstop, three or four times a week. This will make you more fit to participate in any sport.

It isn't hard to set up your own program. If you choose running, get a good pair of running shoes. Make sure you always warm up and then cool down with a number of stretching exercises. You can use these same exercises before you go out and skate. They will increase your flexibility and that's always important.

Any kind of stretching exercise should be done slowly. Avoid quick, herky-jerky motions. In addition, any muscle that is being stretched should be held in the stretched position for fifteen to twenty seconds, longer if it feels comfortable. Never stretch quickly and release. That could cause a pulled muscle.

When you start an exercise, move to the maximum stretch position slowly. You'll feel the muscle stretching, but the feeling should not be painful. At any sign of pain, back off on the stretching motion slowly. A regular stretching program not only strengthens the muscles, but makes them more elastic. That way, you're less likely to suffer a muscle injury such as a pull or tear.

It's a good idea to stretch before you skate and once again after. In fact, if you don't skate for several days, continue your stretching program. It will keep the muscles strong and flexible and keep you in condition.

Stretching exercises for skateboarding should concentrate on the legs and lower back. A basic hamstring stretch is a good way to start. The hamstring is a large muscle running down the back of the leg behind the thigh. A good way to stretch the hamstrings is to stand before a bar or bench about waist-high. Place one leg on the support, keeping it straight. Bend the other leg at the knee ever so slightly.

To do the stretch, lean forward slowly, sliding your hands down the leg that is on the support. As your hands approach your foot, you will feel the hamstring muscle stretch. Hold the position for about twenty seconds, then straighten up slowly. Next, reverse legs and do the same thing again. Both legs can be stretched, alternately, five times.

An exercise that will work both the hamstring and lower back at the same time is called the *hurdler's stretch.* Start by sitting on the ground or the floor with your legs spread apart in front of you. Then fold one leg back, bending it at the knee and tucking it tight to the buttocks. Next, bend forward from the waist, moving your hands towards the outstretched leg. Once again stretch slowly and as far as you can without causing pain. Then hold the position for twenty seconds. As with the previous stretch, reverse your leg positions and do it again. Repeat the stretch five times with each leg.

A basic exercise to stretch lower back muscles is done by lying on a flat surface. Then bend one leg at the knee. Put your hands around your thigh just above the knee and pull the leg up as tight to your stomach as you can without pain. Wait the usual twenty seconds, then repeat with the other leg. You should feel the stretching in your lower back.

You can stretch your calf muscles by standing about two feet from a wall. Place your hands on the wall and move both feet back as far as they'll go while still making full contact with the floor. The further away from the wall you move your feet, the more stretch you will feel in your calves. This exercise can be done with one leg at a time or with both at one time. As usual, hold for twenty seconds and repeat five times.

Quadriceps (the front thigh muscles) can be stretched by holding a rail, wall or chair for balance. Then raise one foot behind you and grab your ankle or lower shin with your hand. Pull your foot back toward the buttocks until your feel the stretching in the quad. Hold twenty seconds, then go the the other leg and repeat five times for each leg.

This is a very basic stretching routine. A coach or even an experienced skater may suggest other exercises that will also help.

In addition, there are a few other long-standing exercises that will help maintain your condition for skateboarding. Stomach muscles (an important muscle group) can be strengthened with old-fashioned sit-ups. Always make sure you do them with your knees bent. Never do a sit-up with your legs straight in front of you. That puts too much strain on the lower back. Strong abdominal muscles, however, will help support the lower back.

It will also pay off to keep your arms and shoulders toned and strengthened. They are an important part of skateboarding, used for balance and for making turns. Upper body standbys are push-ups and pull-ups. They can be done any time and almost anywhere. Even a light weight-training program can be beneficial. Always ask a coach or experienced body builder how to get started and which exercises are best for you.

The exercises that have been outlined above will make anyone more physically fit and make it that much easier to learn how to skateboard. Flexibility and fitness are especially beneficial to the skateboarder as he advances to more technical maneuvers, whether it be streetstyle or on the ramps. So even if the kid next door says that stretching or running isn't necessary for boarding, don't listen. Do it the right way. Being healthy and fit is a matter of lifestyle.

PART THREE

DON SZABO, FRONTSIDE OLLIE AIR AT LOCAL MONTANA RAMP.

LEARNING TO SKATEBOARD

THE BASICS—CRUISING, STOPPING, TURNING

Now it's time to get on the board. Starting up is relatively easy, but there are no shortcuts to advancing, no easy way to do the tricks and maneuvers that you see others doing on the streets and at the skate parks. If you don't start right and pick up the basic skills, you may well get hurt. Remember what Rodney Mullen said about many of today's young skaters:

"I've seen kids begin by trying all kinds of technical tricks on the board. They may end up doing some of the tricks, but they can't really skate at all."

How should you start then? First get that quality skateboard, your helmet, and protective gear. Skaters usually wear sneakers that will give them good traction on the board. Never skate barefooted, no matter what.

You can start on an area where the board won't slide much, like a carpet or grass lawn. Otherwise, begin carefully in your garage, basement, or on the walk or road in front of your house.

Step one is to place your front foot over the front truck of the board and point it straight forward. Then push off with the back foot. When the board begins to glide, bring the back foot up and place it at an outward angle across the back truck of the board. Most skaters will put their left foot over the front truck and push with the right.

Some skaters will put their right foot on the front of the board and push with their left. For years, this has been called *goofy foot* by skaters. There are even a few who put their rear foot on the board first and push with their front. That style isn't very effective, but regular foot or *goofy foot* can produce the same results. It's simply like being right- or left-handed, and some experienced skaters insist that beginners should practice both ways.

Once you've determined which foot is more comfortable as the lead foot and which as the pushing foot, you can begin to move. Start by pushing just once with the rear foot, then placing it back on the board. If you're on a carpet or grass, you won't glide much. If you are on concrete, you'll begin to glide somewhat more, so don't push too hard.

Do this until you feel comfortable bringing your pushing foot from the skating surface to the board. Now you are ready to begin to glide or cruise. You can't really do this on a carpet or grass, so it's time to move to a hard, flat surface. Use the same technique of pushing with the rear foot. Only this time you can push several times to build up cruising speed before bringing the pushing foot back onto the board.

Each skater must eventually find the most comfortable foot position for pushing and cruising. Once cruising, some skaters simply bring the front foot back over the center of the board and keep the pushing foot to the rear. Others prefer to turn sideways with each foot near opposite ends of the board. Then to push again, they must shift their feet into the original pushing position.

There is another style of pushing and cruising that skaters often use

4 PUSHING OFF TO START SKATING.

5 RIGHT FOOT FORWARD SHOWS A GOOFY FOOTER.

when they are covering some real distance on their boards. They will alternate pushing feet. In other words, they will push first with the back foot in the conventional manner. But when they bring the back foot back to the board they place it facing straight ahead instead of at an outward angle. Then they make the next push with the front foot, returning it to the board in its original position.

This back-to-front style continues as they skate down the road or the sidewalk. By alternating their pushing feet, the skater will not tire as fast and will also develop the skating muscles equally in both legs. So it is a good idea to also practice this technique.

Practice your pushing and cruising until you feel very comfortable doing it and also until you feel you have good balance on the board. Try to relax on the board and ride with it. Don't hold your body stiff and rigid. Once you're relaxed you can glide standing straight up, arms and hands out slightly to the sides for balance. Or you might want to bend at the knees a bit and keep your hands out in front of you. This will keep your weight and center of gravity moving forward.

You can experiment with foot placement and with shifting your feet on the board. But don't go too fast. If something goes wrong, you can still hop off the board without falling. Before you pick up speed or cruise down even the smallest of hills, you've got to learn the next lesson: How to stop.

Being able to stop quickly and correctly is a very important part of gaining total control over the skateboard. There are several different ways to slow down and stop. Some skaters favor one over the other way. But sometimes it's the skater's speed that determines the best way to stop.

Pro skater Mike McGill says the best way for a beginner to stop is simply to take his back foot off the board and drag it on the skating surface. That will slow the board enough for the skater to step off. Others simply recommend allowing the board to slow, then stepping off with the back foot while the board is still moving forward. Follow that by stepping off the same side of the board with the front foot. Advanced skaters can kick down on the tail as they step off and have the board pop up so they simply catch it in their hand.

If the board is moving too fast for you to step off and you don't have time to drag your foot, you may simply jump off the board. Jump in the direction your feet or body are facing. This is where physical condition, balance, and knowing how to fall are important. If you are in shape and quick, you should be able to jump off and keep your balance. If you're not in good condition, you could easily pull a muscle by jumping off this way. In addition, if the board is moving very fast, you might not be able to keep your balance when jumping off. If you know how to tuck your shoulder and roll, you won't get hurt.

There are still two other ways to stop a board, both methods often used by more advanced skaters. One way to slow or stop at fast speeds is to make a sharp turn to the right or left. For instance, if you are going down a hill, you can turn and continue until you are facing uphill again. But it takes skill to turn safely at these speeds. You also have to be sure there are no obstacles in the way of the turn or you might end up colliding with something. Using the *power slide,* which is discussed in the section on pool- and ramp-riding, is another way to slow or stop a runaway board.

Then there is the wheelie stop. This is the closest thing to actually having a brake on your skateboard. As you begin to slow down, shift your front foot to the center of the board. Then shift your rear foot to the tail of the board, setting it across the board. When you shift your weight to your rear foot, the front wheels will leave the surface in the conventional wheelie. Put even more weight on the tail and the board will begin to scrape the ground. This braking effect will stop the board so you can step off. If you stop this way often you should put a tail plate or skid plate on your board to protect it from damage.

Stopping is something you should practice immediately. Knowing how

6 THE PROPER WAY TO STOP WITH EASE.

7

to stop and get off the board under different skating conditions can keep you from wiping out or being injured.

The third basic maneuver to learn when first starting to skate is the turn. To be a good skateboarder and to begin doing some tricks and tougher maneuvers you must know how to turn well. That means being very comfortable on the board and being able to go both right and left with relative ease.

According to Mike McGill, a good quality skateboard will turn readily, while it is very difficult for even the best riders to turn well on the cheap imitation boards. With a good board, it is up to the skater who must learn to shift his weight, lean into the turn, and keep his balance.

The trick of turning is to shift the weight of your lower body (legs and hips) into the direction of the turn. As you push and cruise along, your weight is centered directly over the center of the skateboard. You might

8

9 PHOTOS 7–9: PROPER POSITIONING FOR SLALOM TURNING.

want to practice your turns on a very slight downward grade so you can concentrate on the weight shift without having to worry about pushing to keep up your speed. But keep the grade slight. No real downhills.

When you are ready to make a turn, make sure your back foot is facing out, almost perpendicular to the board. Hold your arms out to the side for balance and begin by rotating your shoulders and hips in the direction you want to turn. Then shift the weight in your legs and hips, leaning into the turn. You should begin turning immediately.

The more you lean, the more the board will turn. Don't ever make quick, jerky movements. This can cause a wipeout. All body movements should be smooth and gradual, even when done quickly. Some skaters prefer to lower their bodies by bending at the knees when they turn. This takes practice but may give you better balance when making sharp turns.

The foot placement of each skater can vary to some degree. Some skaters will move their feet to the ends of the board when they turn. Others feel more comfortable with their feet remaining in the center. Shifting the feet for all the different maneuvers is something skaters must practice until it becomes second nature to them. Then, they will do it automatically.

Again, ease into your turning technique slowly and practice going both to the right and left. To come out of a turn, simply shift your weight back to the middle of the board. Bring your hips and shoulders back into cruising position and come out of your lean. The board will begin moving straight forward once again.

Turning is one of the ABCs of skateboarding. No skater can afford to overlook this basic skill if he wants to skate safely and skillfully. So practice turns faithfully. Work on balance, foot placement, turning your shoulders and hips, and the lean. You may lose your balance at first, especially on the sharp turns. But with practice, you'll find that turning is not difficult. Instead of a steering wheel or handlebars, you simply must learn to use your body. And that's really what skateboarding is all about.

BASIC ADVANCED MANEUVERS

Skateboarding is a sport of "doing more." Once a skater masters one skill or maneuver, he invariably wants to move on to another. There probably hasn't ever been a skater who was content to simply push and cruise down the sidewalk day after day after day. So here we go, getting into some of the advanced maneuvers that will give skaters the first steps to more technically complex skateboarding.

After learning to push and glide, stop and turn, one of the first things a skater might try is the wheelie. Remember, a variation of the wheelie can be used to stop the board by scraping the tail on the skating surface.

In a nutshell, a wheelie is any maneuver done with either the front or back wheels of the board off the ground. The secret is balancing your weight over the wheels still in contact with the skating surface. As a rule of thumb, it's easier to do tail wheelies than nose wheelies. That's because skaters pick up balancing their weight over the rear wheels faster than over the front wheels.

The most important part of a wheelie is foot placement. This will lead to the balance needed to complete the maneuver. There are a number of ways to place the feet. It's up to each skater to determine which way is best for him. Once a skater determines his foot placement and begins to wheelie, then all it takes is practice at holding it. Some skaters can wheelie down grades and around turns. Others can spin and turn repeatedly on just two wheels. It's fun, it looks good, and it can be the start of other tricks.

Some skaters prefer to wheelie with both feet at the end of the board. Others will put just one foot at the end of the board and depend on more of a weight shift. To get ready to wheelie, beginning skaters should practice riding their boards on all four wheels using different foot positions. The first is the *hang five* position with five toes of one foot over the front end of the board, the other foot back toward the middle. The second is the

10   THE BASIC KICKTURN.

hang ten, with both feet to the front and all ten toes placed over the end of the board. And the third is the *hang heels* position, with the heels of both feet extended over the back end of the board.

You can wheelie from all three of these positions by simply shifting your weight forward or back. With hang five, the free foot can be used to aid balance. With hang ten and hang heels, the arms, knees and upper body must be used to keep the board balanced on just two wheels.

Once you can skate on all four wheels using these foot positions, it's time to wheelie. First work up to a good cruising speed, maybe even on a slight downward grade. Then shift your feet into one of the above-mentioned positions. Gradually bring your weight back or forward on the board until the opposite set of wheels leaves the ground. Use your arms, knees, and upper body for balance on the hang ten and hang heels. With the hang five, you can also use your free leg.

Try to wheelie as far as you can. If you lose it, start over and try again. Pretty soon, you'll begin to get a better sense of balance and will ride the wheelie longer and longer. A few other tips. When doing the wheelie with a hang-heels stance, balance and the angle of the board can be changed by flexing the ankles. In the one-foot stance (and this can be done at the rear of the board, also), the free leg can sometimes be swung back and forth like a pendulum to help with balance and movement. The arms can also be swung back and forth for more balance.

Even if you like one form of wheelie better than another, try to practice all forms. That would include the one- and two-foot tail wheelie, and one- and two-foot nose wheelie. Some skaters will also squat while doing a front (nose) wheelie. This is more difficult and takes real practice.

Another movement that is often learned about the same time as the wheelie is the *kickturn.* The kickturn is not really used to turn the board, though it could be used in that way. Most times however, it is a rapid-fire maneuver often used to propel the board forward on a flat surface.

The kickturn must be done with one foot on the tail of the board, the other on the nose. When you're ready to begin a kickturn, shift your weight to the back foot and push down enough to raise the front wheels off the skating surface. At the same time, turn your upper body just slightly away from the direction you are going to turn.

Once the front wheels catch air, rotate your body quickly in the direction of the turn. At the same time, the front foot is used to direct the board to the side. This is not a radical turn. The board goes off at maybe a 45-degree angle to the right or left. Then, when the desired angle is reached, the skater shifts his weight to the front, allowing the front wheels to touch down. But as soon as they touch, the weight goes back, the upper body rotates again, and the front wheels come back up. The skater then directs the board to the other side, touching down at the same angle.

By going back and forth quickly, a kickturner can propel the board along a flat surface. The movements must be fast and coordinated. The weight shift, rotating of the upper body, and the quick, up-and-down motion of the front end of the board take a lot of practice. But by mastering the kickturn, you will be a better skater who has another way to propel his board.

Next comes the *360*. This is a trick by which the skater makes a complete turn on his board, finishing by facing the same direction from which he started. The 360-degree turn is done on just two wheels, either the nose or tail. So once again the ability to do the wheelie comes into play. It is also similar to the kickturn, but instead of maneuvering the board just a short distance, the skater must maneuver it in a complete circle.

A good way to begin preparing for a 360 is to do a 180. That's just halfway around. In effect, you are reversing the positions of the nose and tail. For a 180 or 360, some skaters have both feet sideways on the board, positioned near each end. Others keep the back foot sideways, the front foot at about a 45-degree angle. Again, whatever is comfortable is all right.

This maneuver is done with the board either moving or standing still. The skater begins by shifting his feet into the aforementioned position. He then shifts his weight to the back foot and brings the front end of the board into the air. At the same time, he might rotate his upper body slightly away from the direction of the turn so that he can build up momentum.

Once the front of the board is in the air, the skater whips his arms in the direction of the turn, followed quickly by the rotation of the upper body, shoulders and hips. The board will begin turning. Now it takes balance and control by both feet in contact with the board to continue it around in the circle.

At first, you can go for the 180, just turning front to back. Once you maintain balance to do that, take it further and try for the complete 360-degree turn. When you near completion of the turn, just shift your weight forward so the front of the board returns to the skating surface.

A frontside turn means moving in the same direction that the front foot is pointing. A backside turn is made by moving away from the direction of the front foot. The backside is a little more difficult to learn because you're moving backward and can't see where you are going.

The 360 can be done first on the back wheels, later on the front wheels. The same principles apply, only the weight change is reversed. Good skaters can do two or more 360s without stopping. In fact, a skater going around completely two times has just done a 720. Once you feel comfortable with your balance and body movements, there is no limit to the types of spins and turns you can do.

These maneuvers can be used in freestyle and streetstyle skating. By cruising into a 180, the skater will whip around and continue to cruise backward. Another 180 and he is cruising forward again. Or he can do a quick 360 and continue in the direction he was skating.

The 180 kickturn is also used by vertical skaters as a basic turn at the top of a ramp. Just before the skater reaches the top, he uses the same basic kickturn maneuver to reverse the board and allow gravity to begin bringing him down. So the kickturn and spin are valuable maneuvers to master, no matter what type of skating you want to do.

That brings us to the maneuver that might have revolutionized the entire sport of skateboarding. It's called the *Ollie* and is something that is a must for any skater today who wants to do to even more difficult jumps and tricks. It is the Ollie that enables skateboarders to leave a flat surface with all four wheels.

According to skateboarding pro Mike McGill, the Ollie was created by a pro skater named Alan Gelfand, who was from Ft. Lauderdale, Florida. This was in the mid-1980s.

"Alan first did the Ollie in a pool," McGill recalls. "It was like a no-hands air, as they called it at first. He would come up out of the bowl, turn in the air, and come back in without touching the board. He had all four wheels in the air. It was almost ahead of its time."

Before long, the Ollie became the number-one street maneuver, used for all kinds of jumps or whenever a skater wanted to catch air. It's a kind of bang-bang maneuver that takes quickness and coordination, and one that often stumps older skaters.

"I've been skating for thirty years and I still can't Ollie," said former slalom champ Henry Hester. "It's kind of funny, but the older guys can't get it. Yet a young skater today can't ride down the street without doing an Ollie. Guys will Ollie onto a curb and keep going. If you can't Ollie, you have to get off the board to go up on the curb and it will slow you down."

A skater must be moving fairly fast to be able to Ollie. The more speed, the longer and higher the Ollie can be. If you're moving too slowly, the maneuver cannot be done at all. So don't even try an Ollie until you have all the other skills described thus far. You've got to be comfortable on your board and be able to cruise on a flat surface at a good speed. Then, and only then, are you ready to Ollie.

The Ollie is actually two very quick movements, one done right after the other. If the skater's timing isn't right or if he isn't quick enough, the Ollie won't work. So begin with your feet in the normal cruising position, one in front of the other. Work up to speed and have your weight over the center of the board.

To do the Ollie, you must pop the heel of the board down quickly with your rear foot. As the front of the board comes up, push downward with your front foot, shifting your weight to the front as you do. The second motion of pushing the front down (not so much that the wheels touch the skating surface) will cause the rear wheels to lift off, creating a successful Ollie.

The movement, timing, weight shift, and balance of the Ollie demand a great deal of practice. It's hard to believe that the movements just described will bring the board in the air. But today's skaters do some amazing things with the Ollie. They not only jump and turn in the air, but maintain contact with their boards without reaching down to grab them.

If you watch street skaters jump on and off benches, ride handrails, and go over obstacles with their boards, you see them Ollie over and over again. Once you perfect this maneuver and can catch air with ease, you're ready to go into even more advanced technical maneuvers and become a real street skater. And it all begins with the Ollie.

TRACY GAMBRILL, SHOWN UP-CLOSE IN A FRONTSIDE GRINDER.

CRAZY LARRY EXEMPLIFIES A HUGE BACKSIDE OLLIE AIR OVER THE CHANNEL.

"BAD" BRAD GROSS LOFTS A HUGE OLLIE AIR OFF A STREET RAMP.

ADRIAN DEMAIN, SOARING SIX FEET OUT WITH A ONE-FOOT BACKSIDE AIR.

RODNEY MEAD WITH A HUGE STIFFIE INVERT.

STEVE CLAAR SHOWS A TEXTBOOK FRONTSIDE AIR.

AN UNIDENTIFIED SKATER IN AN UNIDENTIFIED INVERTED TRICK.

STEVE CLAAR DEMONSTRATES A FRONTSIDE OLLIE AIR.

ABOVE: VANS TEAM RIDER, STEVE ROYALLE, SHOWN IN A TEXTBOOK AERIAL.

NEAR RIGHT: SCOTT STANTON, SHOWN WITH A HUGE BACK-SIDE AIR.

FAR RIGHT: RODNEY MEAD, FLYING HIGH ABOVE A CARLSBAD HALF-PIPE.

LOCAL ENCINITAS SKATER, CHRIS, LAPS A LOCAL HANDPLANT ON HIS HOME HALF-PIPE.

Top left: RODNEY MEAD SHOWN IN AN ANDRECT HANDPLANT.

Top right: STEVE CLAAR CONTORTING AN INVERT.

Left: RODNEY MEAD WITH A TEXTBOOK INVERT.

ENCINITAS SKATER MIKE MAHER TAIL SLIDES INTO FOCUS ON A CARLSBAD, CALIFORNIA RAMP.

PART FOUR

RODNEY MEAD, NO-FOOT INVERT AT MCGILL'S SKATEPARK

TRICKS, STUNTS, AND RACES

SKATEBOARDING can be a very versatile sport. There are so many things that can be done on a board that it might be tough to choose a favorite. Unfortunately, because of the changing nature of the sport, many of the tricks and races that used to be available to skateboarders have all but disappeared today. The opinion here is that this has hurt the sport.

There is still room for downhill and slalom racing, flatland freestyle, barrel-, and high-jumping. With literally millions of youngsters owning skateboards, the sport should not be limited to the "in" activity, which in the early 1990s was streetstyle skating. For that reason, this section will discuss all styles of skateboarding, even those considered "out" or not cool by today's streetstylers. There is no reason these forms of the sport should not someday surface again.

DOWNHILL AND SLALOM

Henry Hester has described skateboarding in the nineties as an obstacle sport. "Everything is done against a bank or a wall. It's very slow and very technical," he said. Hester, who was a slalom champ and rode down hills as a youngster, said the kids today find no fun in going downhill.

"Kids cruise down a hill three times with the wind blowing in their faces and say, 'well, I did that.' Then it's back to the flats."

But riding a skateboard isn't that different from in-line skating, skiing, and snowboarding. Many skiers use in-line skates to cross-train when there is no snow. And many former skateboarders have taken to the slopes on a snowboard. Snowboarders do downhill and slalom, which makes it even more curious why those two forms of competitive skateboarding have all but disappeared.

Rule number one in downhill skateboarding is to wear all your protective equipment. That's because downhill skating is the most dangerous form of skateboarding. A wipeout at forty miles per hour or more can cause serious injury without any snow to cushion the fall. These speeds can be attained on steep hills by expert skaters. But lesser hills produce lesser speeds and can still be fun.

There was a time when skaters raced downhill, competing against each other for pure speed. In addition, there were cross-country type downhill courses. Mike McGill called them "snake runs," with hills, banks, and ramps. Again, the skaters raced for time.

The technique of riding a hill is similar to downhill racing on skis. In fact, the stance is also similar. Most skaters prefer to place their feet directly in the center of the board. Some will keep both feet parallel, others place one slightly in front of the other.

For downhill skating, it's best to use a board with a long, hard deck.

12   PROPER POSITION FOR A DOWNHILL TUCK.

The wheels should be thin and the trucks wide. This will give the skater more speed and better traction. The basic downhill position is also similar to a downhill skier.

The skater should get into a full tuck position. This means a deep bend at the knees, the upper body bent forward over the knees, head down but eyes forward, and hands out in front for balance. This position will cut wind resistance to a minimum and allow for maximum speed.

Only experienced and talented skaters should attempt steep hills. So if you like speed and want the thrill of racing down a hill, make sure you have absolute control of your board and yourself. Also, know the hill. It's very difficult to stop a skateboard traveling at forty or fifty miles per hour. Know ahead of time just where the hill ends and how you will stop. Practice slowing and stopping at higher speeds. And remember, the potential for serious injury is greater the faster you go. So always think safety first.

Slalom races used to be one of the most popular forms of skateboarding. When Henry Hester began skating in the early 1960s, one of the first things he and his friends did was to paint dots on the street and begin slaloming around them. It was the beginning of a skateboard career that would make Hester a slalom world champion.

"We would probably get up to speeds of about 25 or 30 miles per hour in the slalom," Hester said. "It wasn't fast by downhill standards then, but fast enough so that if you fell you couldn't run it off."

Slalom races were run either on a flat surface with the start down a ramp to give the skaters speed and momentum, or on a slight—five or six percent—downgrade.

"The hill would keep your momentum going and we would speed it up on the turns by gyrating the board by moving our hips forward and back."

The object of the slalom is identical to a slalom in skiing. In fact, that's where the idea came from. The skater must zig-zag around a series of cones as fast as he can. That means a series of sharp, back-and-forth turns while maintaining the maximum speed possible.

There were three main types of slalom competitions—the tight, the giant, and the banked. In the tight slalom, the cones were placed in a straight line. That meant the skater had to make very fast, tight turns one right after the other. The giant slalom saw the cones placed alternately staggered in two lines, making for much wider and sharper turns as the skater went from one line of cones to the other and back again. Banked slalom was on a graded or banked course that was geared for more speed.

Slalom racers normally would choose a flexboard with wide trucks and soft wheels for better traction on the sharp turns. But it still takes a lot of practice before tackling a slalom course at top speed. You can practice the basic technique by making your own slalom course on any flat surface, much as Henry Hester did when he began.

There are two basic stances that slalom skaters prefer. Again, choose the one that feels most comfortable for you and allows you the most maneuverability. The first stance has each foot placed sideways or diagonally at opposite ends of the board. On a thin board, the toes and heels of each foot will extend over the end of the board. The second stance has both feet close together near the center of the board, perhaps a bit closer to the front. The feet are placed diagonally in the same direction. Heels and toes may extend a bit over the end of the board, but not as much as with the sideways stance.

Whichever stance gives you the most speed and most control on the turns is the best for you. Again, there is no right and wrong. It's what works for the individual skater, but these are the two basic stances used by most of the outstanding slalom skaters.

The trick of running a slalom is to cut as close to the cones as possible.

Quick, clean turns are better than slow, wide ones, which will slow you down. The legs and hips will have the primary movement in directing the board. Slalom skaters try to minimize upper body movement. That will slow them down.

Turning is accomplished by leaning and shifting weight, the basic technique discussed earlier. Speed is controlled by hip movement coming out of the turns and by putting weight on the board and then taking it off. Slalom skaters weight the board as they come around the cones. They do this by pushing down hard on the ball of the back foot. Then as they come out of the turn they un-weight the rear with a leg and hip movement. This helps propel the board out of the turn and gets the skater ready to begin the next turn.

Skateboard slalom is rapidly becoming a lost art in the 1990s. The basic techniques outlined above will enable a skater to practice slalom the correct way. Of course, it takes a great deal of practice to even approach the skills of a Henry Hester or other outstanding slalom skaters. Without slalom competition, most skaters are foresaking the skill for streetstyle skating. It doesn't have to be that way. Slalom skating is a lot like slalom skiing. It's fun, exciting, and competitive. And it would be great to see it come back once again.

JUMPING

Jumping on a skateboard has changed dramatically since the creation of the Ollie. In the past, skaters would jump off the board, then come down on a second board or return to their original board. With the Ollie, it is possible to jump with the board, taking it with you as you catch air, then returning to the skating surface while still on the board.

There are a number of ways both the old style and new style of jumping can be used to perform skateboarding stunts and tricks. The Ollie is "in" now, but that shouldn't prevent skateboarders from trying the old ways, either. So once again, we'll talk about both.

A quick example of how the Ollie has changed skateboarding: Before the Ollie, a skater who wanted to go onto a curb would have to do it in two motions. He would approach the curb at an angle, lift the front end of his board in the air by shifting his weight to the rear. As the front of the board cleared the curb, the skater would shift his weight quickly to the front foot, bringing the tail of the board onto the curb. With practice, good skaters could get their boards onto the curb and keep skating. But never did the board catch air.

With the Ollie, skaters can approach the curb, do the Ollie motion described earlier, and catch air with all four wheels as they jump their board onto the curb. The ability to Ollie on and off of objects has changed the face of freestyle skating into streetstyle. Jumping is basic. But some form of it has always been part of skateboarding since the beginning.

Jumping in pre-Ollie days required a board that had some flex in it to cushion jumps, but not enough where the board would bottom out or snap if you landed hard on it. Other basic rules to remember are to start slow and low, and work up to fast and high. That means plenty of practice. And with any jump, good judgement is a must. If you don't feel the takeoff is right or that you can make a perfect landing on the board, then abort the jump. It's better to land on the ground than on the edge of the board. The result could be a turned or broken ankle.

One of the most popular jumps in earlier days was board-to-board jumping. This was simply a matter of jumping from one board to another. It was done by cruising along on one board and jumping to a stationary board that had been previously placed on the surface ahead. It takes timing and concentration, but is a relatively simple jump.

As you approach the second board, work up to the desired cruising speed. The best foot position is almost the cruising position, feet almost parallel and near the center of the board. Get ready to jump by bending at the knees and bringing your arms down. You've got to aim for the center of the second board so you can bring your feet into cruising position immediately.

Flex your knees upward and bring your hands up at the point of takeoff. The trick is not to push out or push too far forward. If you do that, the board you are riding on will simply spring backward and you may not get enough lift or distance to reach the second board. So push up and in the direction of your landing. Land softly, dropping a bit at the knees to cushion the impact. Once you get the technique, you can begin making the jump at greater speeds.

To jump over an obstacle before the days of the Ollie, skaters took off on one board, jumped over the obstacle, and landed on a second board. This, too, takes timing, practice, and strength.

Barrel-jumping was a very popular skateboard activity until recent years. The "barrels" could be anything from the real thing to plastic trash containers to simply cardboard boxes. As with all jumping, barrel-jumpers should be sure to wear all the safety gear available to them, especially a helmet.

The technique of barrel-jumping is similar to board-to-board jumping. The difference is the jumper will be traveling higher and farther in the air. He will not be able to see the landing board until he clears the final part of the obstacle (or last barrel). So he will have just a split second to sight his landing.

Of course, the higher and farther you want to jump, the more speed you will need. You will also need strength and spring in your legs (helped by your arms and shoulders) to get the height and distance to complete the jump. So being in good shape and doing the exercises mentioned earlier will help.

Start with a short and low jump. It's also best to start with a non-solid obstacle, such as a cardboard box, that will give if you hit it. Using a metal trash can or real barrel at the outset could increase the chance of an injury. Center the landing board beyond the final obstacle, far enough from it so you can land in the center. You might want to make a couple of practice jumps without the landing board to get an idea for its placement.

As you approach the jump, work up as much speed as you'll need to clear the obstacles. When you get set to jump, make sure your feet are parallel at the center of the board. Once again bend at the knees and bring your arms down and back so they can help propel you upward and outward. Leave the board just before it is about to hit the first obstacle. Remember not to leave the board too soon and propel yourself forward. If you do that, you'll once again push back too hard on the board and get no height or distance.

In the air, keep it together. Tuck your knees and feet tightly while using your arms for balance. Don't let your arms and legs go every which way because now you have to concentrate on your landing. You'll want to land with both feet together in the center of the second board. So keep them together during the jump.

Try to land with your body erect, not leaning too far backward or forward. Bend at the knees as you hit the board. Once again, you will be landing on a thin board and to miss by even a couple of inches could result in a fall or a turned ankle. Good, flexible body control is all-important. You'll have just a split second to judge your landing or to abort the jump.

Though it was always called barrel-jumping, once you learn the technique and practice, you can certainly jump other objects. It takes skill, athletic ability, and coordination to be a good skateboard jumper. Street-stylers have revived the skill using the Ollie, but it still can be fun to do it the old-fashioned way once again.

13

14

15

A more difficult skill to learn is high-jumping. This is usually done over a bar that can be set at varying heights. The difference in this jump is that the skater will take off and land on the same board. As the skater jumps the bar, the board glides under it and moves into position for the landing. It takes more skill on the part of the skater, because he must control the speed of the board to coincide with the height of the jump. Time to practice again.

To high-jump, the skater must approach the bar straight on. He should not jump until he is very close to the bar. That way he can jump up, not forward. It's important that the jump doesn't alter the course of the board, which must continue rolling straight under the bar.

Many high-jumpers prefer to tuck their legs to the side when clearing the board. The arms should still be up and out after helping to propel the jumper off the board. He must keep his eyes down, watching the course of the board and getting ready for his landing. Again, if you are out of position, try to avoid the board and simply land on your feet. Otherwise, land in the center of the board, bending slightly at the knees as you do.

Today's young skaters use the Ollie for almost all their jumping. That technique was described earlier. Once a skater gets the bang-bang timing of the Ollie, he can jump with the board. The faster he moves, the higher and farther he can jump, the skateboard staying with him. On very long or very high jumps, the skater may reach down and grab the board with one hand, making sure it doesn't fall away from his feet.

So someone who is really good at the Ollie can jump barrels and high-jump while taking the board with them. They don't need a second board. But they do need strength, coordination, timing, and practice. Those qualities are often found in the top streetstyle skaters who use the Ollie every time they get on the board.

POOLS AND RAMPS

Vertical skating—including pool-, bowl-, and ramp-riding—has survived the years better than downhill and slalom. There was much more of this type of skating in the early and mid-1980s because there were so many more skate parks. Skate parks began flourishing in the latter 1970s and into the 1980s. It has only been in the late eighties and into the early nineties that many of them began to close.

There were a number of reasons for the disappearance of the skate park. One is the changing nature of the sport. With the emergence of streetstyle, fewer youngsters were frequenting the parks. Also the price of liability insurance became so high that it put many of the parks out of business.

Skate parks are the perfect place for pool-, ramp-, and bowl-riding. That's because top-quality ramps and bowls can be constructed on the premises with instructors available to show skaters the techniques and form needed to enjoy this exciting form of skateboarding.

Mike McGill is one of the sport's great vertical skaters. He learned and honed his skills at skate parks first in Florida, and later in California. Mike opened his own skate park in Carlsbad, California in 1986 while his parents were running another in Tampa, Florida. But this is the exception, rather than the rule.

"There are really not enough places where kids can go to learn vertical skating," McGill said. "You really need more skate parks because it's difficult for people to make these kinds of ramps in their yards. They're expensive and difficult to construct. There are some YMCAs, Boys' and Girls' Clubs trying to help out, but just not enough free places for kids to learn."

McGill also said that anyone riding ramps or pools should be sure to wear all the protective equipment—helmet, elbow pads, kneepads, and wrist guards.

"Wrist injuries are the most common hurts on the ramps," McGill said.

"But even kids riding handrails and doing stunts like that on the streets wear wrist guards now."

Mike McGill is a world champion in vertical skating, a skater credited with inventing many of the more spectacular maneuvers coming out of the half-pipe ramp. It takes years of dedication and practice to become as good as a Mike McGill, but good skaters with basic skills who are confident on their boards can learn some forms of vertical skating.

Pool-riding became a big fad in southern California where there was an abundance of swimming pools, many of which were constructed with a long curve at the deep end. Many skate parks simulated pools by constructing round and oval-shaped concrete bowls. Those who rode the pools and bowls often always said it was a great thrill and an exciting way to skateboard.

The first thing to remember is how to fall on a ramp or pool. As described in an earlier section, the best thing to do if you lose the board is to drop to your knees and simply slide to the bottom. This means wearing quality kneepads, of course. You should also examine the pool or bowl before you enter, looking for any cracks or bumps in the concrete, anything that might trip you up.

Skaters often use a short board for pool-riding to better help them work the sharp curves. Pool riders like to start low and try to work up to the top edges of the bowl. Some skaters like to grind around the top edge (riding on the trucks or even the deck instead of the wheels) before letting the natural pull of gravity bring them back into the pool and the board back onto its wheels.

It's not easy to describe the various tricks and techniques of pool-riding. The best way to learn is to watch someone do it, then start slowly and gradually, maybe getting some advice from an experienced skater along the way. This is certainly not something beginners should attempt. You should already have very good all-around skating skills before moving into a pool or onto a ramp.

16

17

18

PHOTOS 16–18: MIKE MCGILL SHOWS AN ADVANCED TRICK CALLED THE DOUBLE TRUCK CORNER GRIND.

In riding a pool you've got look at its shape and plan—how to best get to the top edge. You've also got to be sure to attain enough speed so that when you reach the top you won't just stop and have to bail out. With the right speed, you can either continue around, or you can kickturn and come back down. Advanced skaters can grind the edge before coming back.

Pool riders often start at the shallow end, push off to get some speed, then increase it by riding down the slope that goes to the deep end. From there they skate to the part of the pool where the curve is the least sharp and go up as high as they can along the side—to the top if possible—then kickturn and come down again.

If you are skating in a man-made round bowl, then it is easier to keep your momentum. You can either skate in a full circle or go side to side as if it's a half-pipe.

There is one additional technique that pool and ramp skaters should perfect. It's called the *power slide* but is really a sharp, high-speed turn made from a crouched position on the board. The skater will lean so far into this turn that he can put either one hand or both hands down on the skating surface to maintain his balance while pivoting the board. To not use the hands to aid in this type of turn could mean a bad fall. A skater can also use the power slide to stop moving in one direction and quickly reverse to the other.

Ramp- or half-pipe riding can mean simply going up one side, doing a kickturn at the top, coming down, and then going up the other side. But skaters like Mike McGill have perfected some incredible, often spectacular routines coming out of the pipe that almost defy description. They often seem to spend more time in midair than on the skating surface of the ramp. Only the most advanced skaters should try these maneuvers, doing simple things first before working up to the more complex.

Mike McGill also suggests that youngsters wanting to skate vertical should begin slowly.

"Start off on smaller ramps first," he advises. "You can't really begin on a vertical ramp. Then by practicing, watching others, and even looking at skateboard magazines and videos, you can pretty much figure it out.

"The most difficult part for me was trying to keep my speed going up and down. But I was real small when I started and it took me a little longer to get the strength in my legs. But once I got older and the muscles built up, the speed came."

Even a longtime pro like Mike McGill said that building speed and momentum on the ramp was difficult to explain. He likened it to pumping with the legs on a swing, saying the skaters gyrate their legs to keep their momentum going. It seems a matter of weighting and un-weighting again, putting weight on the board as you come down one side of the ramp, then taking the weight off for a second as you start up the other side.

19

20

21

PHOTOS 19–21: MIKE MCGILL WITH A TEXT-BOOK ROCK 'N' ROLL (AN ADVANCED TRICK TO TURN AROUND AND GO BACK THE OTHER WAY).

Once you have this basic momentum, you can begin more advanced maneuvers. The following are just some of the things the outstanding skaters like Mike McGill do during their halfpipe routines.

After a skater becomes proficient at doing a kickturn at the top of a ramp he can begin to catch air. The most basic form is the frontside and backside air. This means coming up out of the ramp, turning in the air and then returning to the ramp facing down.

Catching air is achieved by building up speed and skating right up and off the lip of the ramp. If you are doing a frontside air to the left, that means both your feet will be facing left. You then reach down with your right arm and grab the left side of the board. This move will start the turn. By pivoting with your hips and shoulders you will continue to turn as you come back to the ramp surface. By learning this move, you can begin to work on even more advanced maneuvers.

The backside air simply means turning the board and your body to the right when your feet are facing left. Most skaters still use the right hand to grab the board and then turn the board and their body at the same time. A strong skater gets so high out of the bowl or ramp that even a frontside or backside air is an impressive maneuver.

Many vertical skaters with good gymnastics abilities and upper-body strength will do a handplant at the top of the ramp. This routine takes strength, coordination, and balance. The skater builds up his speed up the ramp. As he approaches the top, he gets down low and begins to turn into the handplant, so that the planting hand is closer to the top of the ramp.

At the top, the skater will reach down and grab the top of the ramp with the planting hand. The other hand will reach down and grab the side of the board. Once the skater grabs the top of the ramp, his momentum will swing his feet up and into the air. The planting arm remains straight and must balance his entire body. His feet come up, but the knees remain bent in the tuck position while the free hand holds the board to the feet.

22

23

24

25

PHOTOS 22–25: MIKE MCGILL ILLUSTRATES THE PROPER WAY TO FALL FROM AN INVERTED TRICK.

A good gymnastic skater can balance at the top of the ramp, holding the plant for several seconds—some even longer—before returning the board to the skating surface. He must be sure to swing his body down onto the ramp, not lose it and fall the other way. This takes outstanding body control. The free hand makes sure the board remains beneath the feet as the skater returns to the ramp and starts down. This maneuver can then be repeated on the other side of the halfpipe and is very impressive. But it obviously isn't for everyone.

A variation of the hand plant is a manuever called the *layback air*. Mike McGill says it was invented by a skater out of Florida named Kelly Lind. Mike is often given credit for inventing it, but he actually just embellished it.

The layback air allows the skater to appear to come out of the bowl or ramp while pivoting in the air to come back down. As the skater approaches the top of the ramp he does the same thing as if he were going to do a full handplant. He reaches down for the lip of the bowl with one hand, while grabbing the front side rail of the board with the other. But instead of going into a full handplant and balancing himself on the lip, he simply uses his hand to help swing the board around and come back onto the ramp to skate down. It's not quite as difficult as the full handplant, but still takes timing and practice.

"I kind of developed a variation to the layback air," Mike McGill said. "When Kelly Lind invented it, he would come up flat. In other words just pivot around with his legs and the board out to the side. I would come out of the bowl upside-down, which meant making a more complete swing of the body and bringing the legs and the board straight up. So my entire body seemed to come out of the bowl, though my hand never left the coping."

Some ramps or bowls have a cutout area on the top called a *channel*, from which the skaters can enter the ramp. Once into the half-pipe, skaters will normally avoid the channel, using it only as a point of entry. However,

PHOTOS 26–29: MIKE MCGILL SHOWS AN INCREDIBLE OLLIE AIR OVER THE CHANNEL OF A HALF PIPE.

some like to use it as a natural place to Ollie while on the ramp. To Ollie over the channel takes practice, but is a nifty maneuver.

The skater must first work up to speed, going up and down the ramp easily. When he's ready to jump the channel, which can be about two feet wide, he has to approach the top of the ramp at an angle. Remember, the Ollie is a no-hands air, so you cannot grab the board as you go over the channel.

If you're approaching the channel from the left side you've got to begin turning the board to the right as you shift your weight to the rear and tap the tail to begin the Ollie. As you shift your weight quickly to the front to catch air, rotate your hips, shoulders, and arms to the right to direct the board over the channel and to make sure you don't sail beyond the rim of the bowl. Keep your body compressed and legs tucked. Gravity will keep your feet in contact with the board.

As you come down and make contact with the ramp, both your body and the board should be facing downward at the same angle at which you approached the ramp. Continue the rotation of your body and arms as you straighten up. That will bring you straight down the ramp and ready to pump up the other side. Good skaters will get high in the air as they Ollie over the channel and clear it easily.

The Ollie is also the basis for a *no-hands air,* another Mike McGill specialty. This maneuver also began in a pool and was later done in the half-pipe. The no-hands air is a means of coming up out of the bowl, totally catching air, and coming back in without touching the *coping* (rim) or grabbing the board.

Again it's a matter of body control and the ability to Ollie high in the air. The skater must time his Ollie near the rim, then begin turn his body and the board at the precise moment all four wheels catch air. The pivot is made in the air—without touching the board—and the skater returns to the surface after doing a 180 and heads back down.

These are just a few of the tricks and maneuvers that can be done on the ramp. To watch a skater like Mike McGill is something to behold. In 1984, for instance, McGill invented a maneuver that Rodney Mullen named the *McTwist*. The McTwist is a 540-degree aerial done in the halfpipe. That means that McGill makes one-and-a-half complete turns in the air before returning to the ramp surface. It's just one of the many incredible stunts that top vertical skaters can do.

Watching a good vertical skater traverse a series of ramps in a skate park is like watching a top athlete perform in any other sport. It can amaze you. They fly through the air, do flips, twists, and handstands. They can balance their boards on the rims or go from ramp to ramp. The number of variations to their maneuvers seems endless. That's why they continue to skate.

"I'm always looking to try new things, just to see if I can do them," one top skater said.

That seems to say a lot about the sport.

FREESTYLE AND STREETSTYLE

Streetstyle skating has grown out of flatland freestyle, which had been a popular form of competition for years. Performed on a flat area with no obstacles, freestyle skaters perfected routines combining many of the skills already mentioned—wheelies, kickturns, spins, handstands, and others. They would perform as many different stunts as they could during a set period of time, with judges looking at style, the difficulty of the routine, originality, and the overall flow.

"Freestyle was the best thing to watch in the middle 1980s," says Rodney Mullen, a world champion. "It was a delicate and static thing, almost like ballet. But in the 1990s, streetstyle has really taken over. In a way, it's sucked the life out of flatland freestyle, which was really inferior to what they are doing now."

That might sound like an unusual statement from a professional skater and world champ, but like many others, Rodney Mullen is very honest about his sport.

"Streetstyle adds strength to freestyle," he explained. "It's like ballet versus football. When it started, it was kind of goofy, just guys launching themselves against obstacles like walls and benches. But gradually it became more technical. Now it's a mixture of strength and obstacles, with a lot of technical stuff. A lot of the street guys can do not only all of my freestyle tricks, but also the ones they've added in recent years."

Anything is fair game in streetstyle skating. It can be a bench, a handrail, a wall, a fire hydrant, a high curb. Streetstylers all know how to Ollie and use the maneuver constantly. They're up and down and all over the place.

There were no obstacles in flatland freestyle. All the tricks that skaters put in their routines were done on a flat surface, or occasionally on a bank or slight grade. Besides wheelies and kickturns, there were 360-degree turns and spins, as well as variations of the Ollie. Skaters who were good gymnasts could do handstands or L-sit maneuvers (balancing upright on their hands with their buttocks off the deck of the board and legs out straight). Some did a V-sit, which was identical to the L-sit but with the legs pointing upward instead of straight out. There were all kinds of variations of these tricks, as well as others, put together in a cohesive, freestyle routine.

Other skaters would do dance-like routines, much like figure skaters do on ice. It's a flowing, gliding routine, combining the movements of ballet with the athleticism of skateboarding.

"I always pretty much knew what I was going to do before I skated," Rodney Mullen said. "Some freestylers tried to make their whole program spontaneous, with no advanced planning, but it never seemed to work that way. Occasionally, I would leave a sequence blank so I could create on the spot, but in a contest I always tried to have a good line and set routine.

"The big thing is to look strong on the board and carry a certain momentum. Then add a few highly technical tricks and a few big, high tricks that aren't too technical."

Streetstyle is more of an anything-goes routine, with any obstacle fair game for a skater. One of the favorite tricks on the streets is handrail riding. A handrail is just what it says, a round metal rail that people hold onto when they walk down a set of stairs. Skaters love to ride the rail. It's a trick that takes skill and balance. So don't take it lightly. A fall from a handrail can be a real wipeout.

A street skater will approach the top of the handrail at a slight angle. He then builds up enough speed to be able to Ollie up onto the rail. Once on the air, the skater balances himself on the board, knees bent and arms out to the side. He then slides down the rail on either the rear truck of the board or on the bottom of the board itself, the deck. The second method takes more delicate balance. It's almost like walking a tight rope. The dismount is the easiest part. Just ride the board off the lower end of the rail, maintaining board contact. Then bend your knees at impact and you'll just keep rolling along to the next obstacle.

Skaters can also Ollie onto the side of a bench and ride the corner the same way they would ride the rim of a pool, letting gravity hold them on the board before the dismount. They also Ollie on and off the side of a wall or building and do all kinds of technical tricks on and off curbs.

Streetstylers can Ollie into the air, then leave the board. They can make the board spin two or three times from side to side, then come back down on it in one smooth motion. Their total control of the board is almost uncanny. Almost all the tricks and stunts they perform utilize the basic skating skills already discussed in previous chapters.

Being a good streetstyle skater takes a lot of practice. As Henry Hester said, streetstylers can work for hours trying new technical routines against a curb or a bench, often not moving more than a few feet. Others still rip down the sidewalks, looking for handrails and other obstacles to conquer.

Unfortunately, this type of skating has taken away some of the overall

30 CHRIS LAMBERT, WITH ONE OF THE MOST DIFFICULT FREESTYLE TRICKS, THE OLLIE TO 360° SHOVE IT. CHRIS IS ONE OF THE FEW SKATERS THAT DOES THIS TRICK WITH THE GREATEST OF EASE.

organization from the sport. There is still slalom and downhill racing in Europe, but contests in the United States have diminished. That doesn't mean skaters can't organize. Just obey the rules of your city or town regarding skating, get your parents to help, and find a place to skate. Then, if you want to concentrate on streetstyle, go ahead and rip it up.

PART FIVE

RODNEY MEAD, NOSEBONE INVERT, CARLSBAD LOCAL RAMP

PROFESSIONAL SKATEBOARDING

DESPITE its uneven history, skateboarding has become a fairly well-organized industry over the years. Though sales of boards and equipment have had their ups and downs along with the sport, there has always been a place for the top skaters. They have become professionals and a number of them have been able to make a nice living from their skateboarding careers.

Professional skateboarders are young men and women, many of whom become pros before the age of twenty and usually retire from active skating by the time they're in their mid-twenties. With streetstyle skating, the dominant form of skateboarding in the early 1990s, there may not be room for as many professionals as in the past. Since there are fewer contests and fewer areas of competitions, there are very few world championships to be won. It may be difficult to determine who the best skaters are.

But for some of the former champs who became pros, skating was a way of life. Let's take a look.

· · ·

Henry Hester, as mentioned earlier, began in the early 1960s on a home-made skateboard. He was one of the pioneers of the sport. When Henry began participating in slalom races in the early 1970s he quickly gravitated to a professional skating career. He was already about twenty-four, older than the pros who followed.

"We would get sponsors," Hester said. "The manufacturers of the boards began paying us to represent them and ride their boards, just as it is now. What we didn't have in those early days were our own board models. I finally had my own wheel and board model, but I was one of a few then. It was like a baseball player having a bat with his name of it. The boards would have our names on them."

Hester also began winning money in contests. He can remember the prizes only being about $1,000 for first place. But that could add up. Eventually, Henry and many of the other early pros found themselves traveling more. They went to Europe and raced there. Downhill and slalom were popular in many parts of Europe, especially where skiing was popular, because the races were so similar.

"I won a lot of races in those days and I was finally declared the world champion in the slalom," Hester explained. "I had that title for about four or five years. After that, I started a series of my own contests called the Hester Series. We held contests in pools and in skate parks and we would get money from our sponsors."

Hester said that when he first turned pro there were only about twenty-five or thirty world-class slalom skaters and maybe the same number of freestylers. There were no more than eighty or so pros when he skated and he says there weren't a whole lot more in the early 1990s. So it's a rather closed fraternity.

Henry Hester feels that many of the skaters in the early 1990s aren't as competitive as those who came before.

"A lot of skaters downplay the competitive part of the sport," he said. "They skate for themselves and get personal satisfaction out of being able to do a certain trick or technical maneuver. The camaraderie is still there, but it's more subtle."

For Mike McGill, it all started on a borrowed board in his home state of Florida when he was nearly twelve. But he learned and progressed rapidly. When he was just fifteen, he had $421 in the bank and decided to go to California during Christmas vacation.

"I was already doing the layback air," he recalls, "and at the time no one in California had seen it. A lot of photographers took pictures of me and they got into all the skateboarding magazines. This was in 1979. A couple of manufacturers contacted me and put me on their teams.

"I was what they called a sponsored amateur then. I wasn't paid. But I began traveling all over Florida to different contests, then would fly back to California every three or four months, competing in vertical contests and spending my summers there. I skated all the parks that were springing up then and this was my routine for two or three years."

It was the beginning of a skating life for Mike McGill. While still an amateur he traveled to Sweden, where he was an instructor at summer skating camps, still representing a board company. In 1981, he was named one of the top amateurs in the country and began entering professional contests. In those days, amateurs could compete against the pros and still remain amateurs.

"In 1982 I had my first board model," he said. "I designed it myself, the shape, the kind of trucks I wanted, everything. Unfortunately, skateboarding was in one of those dead periods when the board came out. And when I turned pro about the same time, we were only getting about $150 for winning a contest. But the money didn't have much significance for me then. It was more important that I reached my goal of being a champion and having my own board."

But by 1984, skateboarding was experiencing a revival and Mike McGill was enjoying all the benefits of being a professional. He began making videos, had a new board model, and began traveling all over the world.

"We went to Sweden and Japan and began making good money with our boards," he said. "Eventually we began giving demos all over Europe, in Australia, and even Norway. Skating has remained popular in Europe. Most of the kids there don't play baseball or American football. It's either soccer or nothing. So there aren't a lot of freedom sports and skateboarding was something the kids could do on their own."

Mike McGill has continued to make skating his life. He moved to California for good in 1986 and opened his own skateboard park and shop. His parents run another in Florida. He is still looked upon as one of the best vertical skaters in the world and will accept a challenge from anyone at his own park. And because of the stunts and tricks that he has created, Mike McGill is a skateboarding legend in his own time.

Rodney Mullen has had to watch the style that made him a champion become obsolete. Flatland freestyle, of course, has been largely replaced by streetstyle. But Rodney is still considered one of the greatest skateboarders ever.

He had to almost beg for his first skateboard because his doctor father thought the sport was too dangerous. But when he received it in January of 1977, he never looked back. Admitting that he started skating because it was a "cool thing to do," Mullen found he took to the sport quickly.

Before long, he was being sponsored by little shops in Florida and in a few months was entering contests. Within two years, he won the amateur freestyle championship of California.

"In 1980, when I was thirteen I won the big world championship," he said. "I was a freestyler and at the time it was very big. I got a lot of magazine coverage and was picked up by a major sponsor. So my life changed, but skating was beginning to die out again and not that many people noticed."

By 1985, skateboarding went into another boom period and Rodney Mullen continued to win freestyle titles and contests. He had graduated high school in 1984 and soon after began going out on tours, giving demos as a representative of the manufacturer.

"By 1986, skateboarding was huge again and we were all stars," Rodney admits. "It wasn't always an easy thing for me to go through because I was very shy at the time. But I started to see a lot of the world. We went to Europe and other places. Looking back, the traveling was one of the best parts of it for me."

As happens in some other sports, Rodney Mullen experienced what too much skateboarding can do. He finally suffered a kind of burnout.

"I was always very intense," he said. "By the time I started winning I was doing about five hours of intense skating a day. I knew guys who would actually skate all day and never get real good. But I concentrated. What happened is I reached a point where I wasn't enjoying skating anymore. It was too much. So I kind of mellowed out and started skating just a few hours a day and having more fun with it."

Looking back at his own skating career, Rodney suggests that skateboarding should always be fun and not a duty.

"It was the guys you never see and who work on their own who suddenly show up and do all the tricks. But everyone should have fun. I also tell guys to be a little different, not to blend in. I look for guys who are original, who think about what they do and then add a little bit. If I put them on the team it's because they aren't like everyone else."

"The companies still put their money into certain kids. I've seen kids of thirteen, fourteen, or fifteen making several thousand dollars a month as pros. When it was big in the middle eighties some of us were making up to ten thousand a month. That's kind of heavy for a young kid. But I can remember my dad changing his tune about skateboarding. He went from saying I was turning into a bum and a derelict to, 'wow, that's the greatest investment I ever made.' "

As a pro in the early 1990s, Rodney Mullen continues to give a lot of demos. He also enjoys helping skaters on amateur teams.

"There's a lot of pressure on these guys being in the public eye for the first time," he said.

He continues to design products for his sport and enjoys working with a company. Since boards and wheels change so quickly, there is always a search for ways to improve and modify equipment.

"You stay busy because in skateboarding things can become obsolete in just a few months," Rodney Mullen said.

That seems to be the biggest thing in skateboarding, to keep up with the ever-changing trends. A skating life is certainly not for everyone, but the three pros represented here all found ways to make the most out of the talents they honed on the streets, the sidewalks, and in the skate parks. They not only competed and became champions, but also became involved in spreading the skateboarding gospel through clinics, demonstrations, and videos. In addition, they became involved in the design and manufacturing of skateboarding equipment.

It's hard to say whether the same opportunities will be available for future professionals. With fewer contests, fewer titles to win, and the domination of streetstyle, the sport continues to change. Unfortunately, the change hasn't always been for the better. This is not to diminish the skills and dedication of today's skaters. They are highly skilled, almost incredible in the maneuvers they manage on that small piece of wood with the attached wheels.

But skateboarding needs more organization. It also needs a return to some of the earlier disciplines. Streetstyle is probably here to stay. But downhill and slalom competitions were exciting and well organized before they faded. There is really no reason why they can't return. Those events have never disappeared from the ski slopes. In a sense, they belong in skateboarding, too.

Vertical skating is dynamic, exciting, and highly athletic. Yet with the disappearance of many skateboard parks it, too, is on the wane. This is another aspect of skating that should survive. Just watch a skater like Mike McGill soaring out of the half-pipe and you'll see why.

For nearly thirty years, skateboarding has been governed by the whims and nuances of the next crop of young skaters. Maybe it's about time for the sport to take charge and encourage new skaters to try all forms of the sport. What better spokesmen than champions like Henry Hester, Mike McGill, and Rodney Mullen? They are only three of many who have loved skateboarding and devoted years of their energies to it.

Lastly, this book has tried to cover all aspects of skateboarding, giving the reader a soup-to-nuts approach to the sport. Don't reject any one form of skating just because the kids down the street or at your school tell you it isn't cool or isn't the "in" thing to do. If you get on a board, learn the basic skills and have an adventurous spirit, then go for it, any way you want.

GLOSSARY

Aerobic fitness—A state of fitness marked by an increase in heart and lung conditioning that is achieved by increasing the body's efficient intake of oxygen.

Backside air—A midair turn, usually done coming out of a ramp or half-pipe. The backside air is made in the direction opposite that which your feet are facing on the board.

Backside turn—Any turn made in the direction opposite that which your feet are facing on the board. If the feet are facing right the backside turn is made to the left.

Barrel-jumping—An older skateboard discipline that involves jumping over a row of barrels, cans, or even cardboard boxes. Besides jumping the obstacle, the skater must land on a second board placed at the end of the jump.

Catching air—Any skateboard maneuver in which all four wheels of the board are off the skating surface at the same time.

Channel—A cut-out area on the top of a ramp or bowl from which the skaters can enter the ramp. Some skaters like to use the channel as an obstacle to Ollie across while skating in the ramp.

Crossover sport—Any sport that incorporates some of the skills needed to start a new sport or practice an old one. Many surfers, for instance, use skateboarding as a crossover sport, while many skateboarders, in turn, take up surfing.

Deck—The name given to the top surface of a skateboard.

Downhill—A form of racing from skateboarding's earlier days. It is similar to downhill racing on a ski slope, the contestants trying to get to the bottom of the hill in the fastest time.

Flatland freestyle—A competitive discipline characterized by a series of tricks and maneuvers done on the skateboard while on a flat surface, such as a skating rink. Contests are judged on style and originality of the program. This discipline has been largely replaced by streetstyle skating.

Frontside air—A midair turn, usually done coming out of a ramp or halfpipe. The frontside air is made by turning in the direction in which your feet and body are facing on the board.

Frontside turn—Any turn made in the same direction your feet are facing on the board. If the feet are facing right, the frontside turn is made to the right.

Goofy foot—A term given to skateboarders who put their right foot on the front of the board and push off with their left. There is actually nothing wrong about skating in this manner.

Half-pipe—The name given to a pair of ramps placed opposite each other and allowing the skater to come down one and skate up the other. Half-pipe competition has always been a big part of vertical skating.

Handplant—The act of balancing on one hand at the top of a ramp or bowl. The skater who has the strength and balance to do a handplant can then make several different turns and maneuvers from the basic plant.

Hang five—One pre-wheelie position of the feet that has the five toes of one foot over the front end of the board with the other foot back toward the middle.

Hang heels—This pre-wheelie stance has the heels of both feet extended over the back end or tail of the board.

Hang ten—Another pre-wheelie stance with both feet at the front or nose end of the board and all ten toes set over the end of the board.

High-jumping—A former skateboarding discipline rarely done by today's skaters. It usually describes jumping from the board over a bar and then landing on the board as it glides under the bar.

Hill riding—A term used to describe skating up and down hills.

Kick—A term used to describe the slight rise at the nose or tail end of the skateboard. Some boards have a single kick, others have a double kick, or a rise at both ends.

Kickturn—A basic maneuver used mostly to propel the board forward on a flat surface. It is done by raising the front wheels off the surface and pivoting the board 45 degrees in one direction, then quickly pivoting it 45 degrees in the other direction. The same technique can be used to turn the board 180 or 360 degrees, or even more.

Layback air—A vertical skating maneuver in which the skater does a partial handplant at the top of a ramp or bowl and swings his body and the board around in the air before returning to the skating surface for the trip down.

L-sit—A freestyle maneuver in which the skater balances himself upright on the board with his hands. The buttocks are raised off the deck of the board, and the legs held together and straight out.

McTwist—An acrobatic vertical maneuver done in the half-pipe and named after Mike McGill. The McTwist is a 540-degree aerial, or one and one-half complete turns in the air before returning to the ramp surface. It requires a great deal of skill and much practice, and is not a maneuver for beginners.

No-hands air—This is a vertical skating maneuver in which the skater catches air at the top of a ramp or bowl and then returns to the skating surface without touching the rim of the bowl or grabbing the board.

Nose—The name given to the front end of the skateboard.

Ollie—Perhaps the most important maneuver in today's streetstyle skating, the Ollie is the way skaters get their boards into the air. It takes timing, coordination, and practice to make the two quick moves (popping the heel of the board down, then shifting weight quickly to the front) in succession that will enable the skater to catch air. Street skaters use the Ollie constantly.

180—A half-turn on the board that will enable a skater to turn from front to back. It can be done frontside or backside, and in several different ways.

Power slide—A sharp, high-speed turn in which the skater will lean so far to one side or the other that he will put one or both hands down on the skating surface to maintain his balance. The power slide is often used on a ramp or hill when the skater wants to stop moving in one direction and quickly reverse to the other.

Slalom—A skateboarding race in which the skater must guide his board around a series or line of specially placed cones. It is similar to the slalom races in skiing, but isn't really done much by today's skateboarders.

Streetstyle—The name given to the most popular form of skateboarding of the early 1990s. Streetstyle skaters love to jump obstacles, ride over handrails and benches, go up and down off walls, ride stairs, and take up the challenge of every obstacle in their path. Though streetstyle is often bold, it can also be very technical.

Swellbow—A slang term used to describe a swelling condition in the elbow that can result from too many falls off a board. A good set of elbow pads will enable a skater to avoid getting a swellbow.

Tail—Term used to describe the back end of the skateboard.

360—A complete turn on the skateboard that leaves the skater facing the same direction from which he started. A 360 can be done several ways, on a flat surface, on a ramp, or completely in midair.

Truck—The name given to the metal suspension system on a skateboard. Well-made trucks include built-in shock pads to absorb impact and will also respond to the skater's weight shifts and turns freely.

Vertical skating—General term used to describe skating in a bowl, half-pipe, pool, or ramp. One of the most popular skateboarding disciplines of the mid-1980s.

V-sit—A freestyle maneuver similar to the L-sit in that the skater supports his weight with his hands and raises his buttocks off the deck of the board. With the V-sit, he holds his legs straight and pointing upward instead of straight out.

Wheelie—A basic skateboard maneuver done with either the front or the back wheels of the board off the ground. The wheelie takes good balance and is the basis for more advanced freestyle tricks.

ABOUT THE AUTHOR

BILL GUTMAN has been a freelance writer since 1972. In that time, he has written more than 100 books, many of them in the sports field. His work includes profiles and biographies of many sports stars, including recent works on Bo Jackson, Michael Jordan, David Robinson, and Magic Johnson. In addition, Mr. Gutman has written biographies of such non-sports personalities as former president Andrew Jackson and jazz immortal Duke Ellington.

He has also written seven novels for youngsters—many of which have sports themes—as well as specialized high-interest low-vocabulary books. His adult books include the Magic Johnson biography, *Magic, More Than a Legend*; an autobiography with former New York Giants baseball star Bobby Thomson, and re-creation of the 1951 Giants-Dodgers pennant race called *The Giants Win the Pennant! The Giants Win the Pennant!*; a collection of profiles of former major league baseball stars called *When the Cheering Stops*; as well as several basketball and baseball histories.

Prior to *Skateboarding*, Mr. Gutman has written instructional "how-to" books on thirteen different sports in a series entitled *Go For It!* He currently lives in Poughquag, New York, with his wife, Cathy, two stepchildren, and a variety of pets.